THE CASE *of* MISTRESS MARY HAMPSON

THE CASE *of* MISTRESS

MARY HAMPSON

Her Story

of MARITAL ABUSE

and DEFIANCE

in SEVENTEENTH-

CENTURY ENGLAND

Jessica L. Malay

Stanford University Press   Stanford, California

Stanford University Press
Stanford, California

Printed in the United States of America on acid-free, archival-quality paper

Library of Congress Cataloging-in-Publication Data

Malay, Jessica L., author.
 The case of Mistress Mary Hampson : her story of marital abuse and defiance in seventeenth-century England / Jessica L. Malay.
    pages cm
 Includes bibliographical references.
    ISBN 978-0-8047-8628-7 (cloth : alk. paper) -- ISBN 978-0-8047-9055-0 (pbk. : alk. paper)
 1. Hampson, Mary, 1639-1698--Marriage. 2. Abused wives--England--Biography. 3. Wife abuse--England--History--17th century. 4. Marriage--England--History--17th century. I. Hampson, Mary, 1639-1698. Plain and compendious relation of the case of Mrs. Mary Hampson. Contains (work): II. Title.
    CT788.H275M35 2014
    942.06092--dc23
    [B]

                        2013038765

Designed by Bruce Lundquist
Typeset in 11/15 Centaur MT at Stanford University Press

FOR NANCY AND MARIANNE
in thanks

CONTENTS

ILLUSTRATIONS

ACKNOWLEDGMENTS

Mary Hampson's story is very much about the communities and individuals who helped Mary throughout her life. I have also received help from many communities and individuals during my work on Mary Hampson. This book would not have come into being without the vision and encouragement of Emily-Jane Cohen, who saw in Mary's story the potential to engage a wide audience with Mary's gripping tale. Her guidance as this book took shape has been invaluable. The University of Huddersfield's School of Music, Humanities, and Media funded much of the research for this book, including work in the National Archives and the Huntingdonshire Library and Archives. The staff at both these archives were always helpful and generous with their time. Special thanks go to Celia Pilkington, the archivist at the Inner Temple, for allowing me to view their collection and for providing generous assistance. Nancy Skewis was involved in this book at an early stage, offering useful suggestions throughout the writing process. I must also thank David McNulty for his encouragement and constant interest as Mary Hampson's story unfolded.

A CHRONOLOGY
of the LIFE *of* MARY HAMPSON

1627 Birth of Robert Hampson.

1639, August 5 Birth of Mary Wingfield later Hampson.

1656, August Marriage of Mary Wingfield and Robert Hampson.

1657, April 15 Birth of Elizabeth, first child of Robert and Mary.

1658, July 7 Birth of son Robert.

1658, Autumn Fight between Robert and his sisters. The Hampsons move out of the Holborn Road house, into rooms near Somerset House in central London.

1662, January 29 Birth of daughter Mary.

1663, Summer Robert beats and abandons Mary. She moves to Richmond in Surrey.

1663, October Birth of daughter Anne.

1664, May or June Mary leaves for France.

1664, August Death of Mary's uncle, John Whalley.

1666, April Mary returns from France and lodges with the Terry family.

1666, July 16 Death of daughter Anne.

1666, September 2 Great Fire of London. Robert's Inner Temple chambers destroyed.

1667, Spring   Mary and Robert move to Robert's new Inner Temple chambers.

1668, February   Mary and Robert Hampson reconcile after a four-day fight in January and move to lodgings in St. Martin's Parish, London.

1668, Summer   Mary and Robert move to a house in New Southampton Square.

1669, September   Death of Mary's mother, Elizabeth Whalley Wingfield.

1669, December   Robert leaves Mary and moves to Exeter House.

1670, February 1   Robert locks Mary out of the New Southampton Square house.

1670, February 28   Robert has Mary's servant Katherine Brown arrested and brings Mary in front of the justice of the peace.

1670, March   Court of Arches case commences.

1670, June   High Court of Delegates case commences.

1671, May   Mary leaves for France after agreeing to a separation from Robert.

1673, November   Mary returns to England to secure her alimony.

1673, December   Edmund Everard arrested; accuses Mary of trying to poison Robert.

1674, January   Mary called before Secretary, Lord Coventry to answer Everard's accusations that she tried to kill Robert.

1674–1677   Mary is living in France.

1674, December   Robert claims Mary is dead.

1677   Mary comes to England for a short time and then returns to France.

1680, Spring   Mary returns to England to sue Robert for her alimony.

1680, May   Mary's suit against Robert for nonpayment of alimony is heard; Mary travels to Amsterdam.

1680–1682   Mary is living in the Netherlands.

1681   Elizabeth Hampson marries Charles Bill.

1683–1692   Mary lives in Paris and possibly in the Netherlands.

1684   Mary publishes *A Plain and Compendious Relation of the Case of Mrs. Mary Hampson* (two editions).

1685   Robert publishes *A Relation of the Design of Mrs Mary Hampson*

1688, December   Robert dies and is buried in the Inner Temple.

1692   Mary returns to London.

1698, February 15   Mary dies in the parish of St Bride, London.

Hampsons of Taplow, Buckinghamshire

Sir Robert Hampson m. Katherine Good
(4 children including Sir Thomas)

Sir Thomas Hampson m. Anne Duncombe

Thomas m. Mary Dennis

Robert m. Mary Wingfield

George m. Grace Holte

Mary m. John Lawrence

Rebecca m. Ambrose Benet

Margaret m. Sir Giles Hungerford

Ambrose, unmarried

Katherine, unmarried

Elizabeth, unmarried

FIGURE 1. Hampson and Wingfield Families.

Wingfields of Kimbolton Castle, Cambridgeshire

Sir James Wingfield m I. Elizabeth Brakyn
                      (4 children including Sir Edward, the heir)

            m 2. Elizabeth Bodenham
               (5 children including Bodenham)

Mr Bodenham Wingfield m. Elizabeth Whalley

Elizabeth (died an infant)

Mary m. Robert Hampson

Robert Hampson m. Mary Wingfield

Elizabeth m. Charles Bill

Robert (died an infant)

Anne (died at six)

Mary unmarried

Introduction

EARLY MODERN MARRIAGE
and the CASE *of* MRS. MARY HAMPSON

One cold night in January 1668, after two days of arguments and beatings, a lawyer named Robert Hampson held a pistol to his wife Mary's throat. The man Mary would later describe as a "monster" appeared to be contemplating a permanent end to their marital problems. This was not the first episode of violence in the Hampson marriage, nor the only time that Mary's life was in danger. But it was certainly one of the most traumatic experiences she underwent. Robert would later claim he intended only to frighten Mary, while she testified in compelling detail that the pistol was charged with powder and shot.

Even after Robert Hampson abandoned Mary in late 1669, Mary was forced to endure frequent episodes of violence at her husband's instigation. These included being forced from her home by an armed gang, thrust into a violent mob by Robert's clerk, and stalked by a nefarious spy. Those men and women brave enough to help her were insulted, at times beaten, and in one case imprisoned. Mary recounts these, and many other, harrowing episodes during her thirty-two-year marriage to Robert Hampson in a pamphlet first published in 1684. In this autobiography Mary attempts to come to terms with the injustice of her marriage, and her society's inability—or unwillingness—to protect her. She justifies her actions and asserts her honor and virtue by framing the conflicts in her marriage in the terms of a struggle between good and evil. In her story she emerges as the heroine of often-terrifying experiences.

When reading Mary's story for the first time, it is difficult to contain one's outrage, so effectively does she present her case. However, her version is only one of several accounts of the Hampson marriage, and these offer more shocking and conflicting details. The other stories of this marriage, mostly found in legal documents, place Mary's autobiographical account in a much richer context. Here the events of this marriage are shown to be more complicated, and the violence more intense, than Mary recounts in her pamphlet. In these legal documents we also see Robert Hampson defending his actions. Through his defense we are able to form a more complete picture of his character and motivations. We hear the voices of Mary's daughters in their court testimony and learn how their parents' conflicts affected them. The Hampsons also appear in other pamphlets in which Mary is accused of criminal behavior. And in one small corner of a church is a stone engraved with unique evidence of a moment of shared unity between the couple. Through all these sources a more nuanced and complicated portrait of this marriage emerges than is at first evident in Mary Hampson's own retelling.

Marriage in this period was not a private matter, but an institution in which there was heavy social investment. The household, through the marital bond, was seen as a bulwark of social stability. A quiet home was believed to foster a quiet community. Because of the centrality of marriage within society, the arrangement of marriages involved not only family members but often members of the wider community. These neighbors also maintained surveillance on appropriate marital behavior and appear to have been eager to report moral irregularities. Mary Philpott told the authorities that she looked through a chamber window and saw William Atkins "come from the bed of John Knoth's wife." Joan Whitehead saw through a crack in the wall her neighbor Dorothy Buck with another man "when her husband was out of town." George Mathews, who rented a room from the shopkeeper Edmund Alden, reported seeing Alden with another man's wife.[1]

Although these examples seem very like the actions of a peeping Tom, they were part of an understanding of community that included maintaining social harmony. This inevitably meant, in an era of no divorce, policing the activities of married couples. These activities named and shamed, as well as bringing erring couples into court for further punishment. This served not only to correct offenders but also to warn others to avoid such transgressions. However, along with bringing to light and discouraging sexual misbehavior, the surveillance also policed other activities that disrupted marital harmony—most especially marital violence.

Unfortunately, unlike sexual misbehavior, the definition of marital violence in this period was not so fixed. This is because seventeenth-century English society tolerated a certain degree of household violence. It was believed that from time to time physical chastisement was an essential corrective to a wayward wife, child, or servant. Much of Robert Hampson's justification for his violence toward Mary was based on this belief. However, excessive rather than corrective violence was seen as disruptive and was thus condemned, though the definition of excessive violence was always fluid. It was in cases of what a community collectively defined as excessive violence that interference was considered not simply acceptable but necessary. Violence was considered excessive when it threatened to permanently damage or kill a woman. Thus when George Wilkinson began beating his wife with a cane outside Kennington Church in London, people came out of their houses to intervene. William Bullocke had to face the fury of the crowd he attracted while beating his wife.[2] In another instance, a young gentlewoman named Anne Dighton was supported by a couple when staying at the Earl of Lincoln's house in London. In the middle of the night, Mary Morrante found Anne crying and brought her to her room. Thomas Dighton threatened to beat both Mary and her husband if his wife did not return to their room. Anne, hoping to avoid further humiliation, went with her husband, who commenced beating her. By the end of the night the Earl of Lincoln and some of his household men had to intervene, resulting in a violent altercation among several of them.[3] These examples show the willingness of the community to physically interfere in an effort to restore social order, but they also illustrate what communities sought to avoid with earlier interventions of a less disruptive nature.

There is much evidence of members of a community mediating marital difficulties with advice, chastisement, written agreements, monetary incentives, and social disapproval.

Ironically, one of the social mechanisms designed to encourage marital harmony was often the catalyst for both early marital conflict and long-term personal misery. This was the legal state of coverture into which all English women entered upon marriage. Under coverture, the wife was covered or subsumed within the legal identity of her husband. In the strictest legal definition of coverture, the wife had no separate existence but was conjoined with her husband. Under coverture a woman had no rights to any personal items, to her children, to any income, or to any inherited goods that came to her during the marriage; all belonged to the husband.[4] As Robert Callis explained in 1648, "It is clear that all Chattells personall, as ready Mony, Plate, Jewels, Apparell, Horses, Kine and other goods of like nature, which a woman brings with her in marriage, or which she hath given to her during coverture, is vested in the Baron" or husband.[5] Note that here even a woman's clothes are in this list, and it was not unusual in marital conflicts for a woman to be thrust out of her house with only the clothes on her back. Legally, the husband could demand these as well. He owned all of a woman's personal property in life and could dispose of it as he chose when he died. One of the more bizarre bequests found in wills from the period is that of the husband who leaves a wife her clothes.

In other European countries, the situation for married women was not quite so bleak; a married woman maintained some legal rights to her property after marriage. In seventeenth-century France, a woman could be awarded a separate estate solely for her use, one in which her husband had no rights. Interestingly, women in most European countries, including Scotland, did not take the husband's family name but retained their maiden name. A woman took on the husband's surname in England because again, under coverture, she became one with the husband—her legal rights subsumed as well as her very identity.[6] By the nineteenth century, marriage reformers called the legal practice of coverture civil death.[7]

The Married Women's Property Act of 1870 provided some relief from coverture's worst aspects, though even this legislation was flawed, and many women continued to suffer under restrictions of coverture well into the twentieth century.

Despite its harshness, legal and moral commentary in the sixteenth and seventeenth centuries justified the English practice of coverture by insisting that only through coverture could a healthy marital partnership be maintained. They argued that coverture ensured couples worked together for the common good of their household, rather than for their own, possibly competing, financial and personal interests. The sacrifice of the wife's autonomy was seen as justified for the good of the entire household and ultimately in the woman's best interest. Moralists especially excused the "covering" of the wife by the husband, by insisting this was akin to God's protective coverture that, according to Robert Bruce, "covereth our wickednesse [that] we may stand in his presence, & be defended from the divel and all enemies."[8] Edward Reyner further explains this functioning of coverture, inviting the reader to associate a husband with Christ:

> [A husband's] Duty is protection of his wife from wrongs and dangers, to rescue her, if in jeopardy (as David did his wives) and to right her. . . . Boaz was to take Ruth into his protection as the hen her chickens under her wings, signifyed by spreading his skirt over her, that she might be safe under the wings of her husband. A man giveth Coverture.[9]

Or as Reyner puts it even more succinctly, "The wife is the weaker vessel therefore she must be carefully and gently handled, as a chrystal glass."[10] Thus, through marriage a man and a woman were seen to be rightly conjoined as one male entity, or again as Reyner writes: "Mariage is a moral conjunction of two persons, so as Man and wife are in Law one flesh by Gods Ordinance."[11]

The contradictions emerging from this legal and moral fallacy, which insisted two individuals could blend into one entity of identical interests, was visible throughout the culture—in households, public spaces, and even the theater. The anxieties and conflicts that shot through society regarding marriage provided rich source material for dramatists. In November 1680 Robert Hampson was treated to a production of John Fletcher's domestic comedy *Rule a Wife and Have a Wife* (first performed in 1624) performed for the lawyers of the Inner Temple, one of the Inns of Court in London where Robert had his chambers. This play was part of a long tradition of marital comedies that drew on established gender roles and the inequity in early modern marriage. In *Rule a Wife and Have a Wife*, as in its much more famous precursor *Taming of the Shrew*, the socially unacceptable behavior of the wife has to be corrected by the husband in the interest of marital harmony and social order. The leading character, Leon, puts this most clearly when he tells his rich new wife, Margarita, that "wives are reckoned in the rank of servants" and that although before marriage she may have owned her own house, after marriage he tells her brutally that now "I am lord of it, I rule it and all that's in it; you have nothing."[12] This is the same lesson Petruchio teaches Kate in *Taming of the Shrew* through starvation and intimidation. Women, she tells her companions, "are bound to serve, love and obey."[13] The schooling of a "shrew" or disobedient wife was a common subject in comedy throughout the period and played on the tensions found in real-life marriages.[14] Robert Hampson no doubt watched the taming of Margarita on that November evening in 1680 with wistful relish, seeing his brutal behavior toward Mary through the lens of comedy. In these comedies, the abuse visited on the wife is emptied of its horror through the dramatic convention of submission and reconciliation.

In reality there was no comedy to be found in the plight of the abused wife, as can be seen in the experience of Cecily Jackman. Her husband, John, threw her out of the house with only ten shillings and "a paier of hose or shoes scarse worth the wearing."[15] In a more famous marital conflict, between Richard Sackville and his wife, Anne Clifford, Richard imprisoned Anne in his country house. In addition he took their daughter away from Anne and placed her in the care of his own relatives. He did this in an attempt to force Anne to sign away her interest in the vast northern lands of her father in exchange for a large financial settlement. Anne wrote in her autobiography that her husband "used fair means and persuasions and sometimes foul means" to force her obedience.[16] Her second husband, Philip Herbert, was even more abusive. Anne wrote in a letter that she could not come up to London without his permission for fear "he should take that occasion to turn me out of this house as hee did out of Whitehall, [where they had lived] and then I shall not know where to put my head."[17] Another Anne (Wentworth) so feared her husband that in her autobiography she wrote "*He* has in his barbarous actions towards me, a many times over-done such things, as . . . [would] be one day judged a murdering of [me] . . . I was forced to fly."[18]

These examples reveal a broad distance between comedy and reality and the real implications for women from the legal practice of coverture, which rather than being the instrument of marital harmony was often the catalyst for marital abuse. This reality was recognized by parents and relatives of soon-to-be-married women. But rather than pursuing a change in the legal status of married women through legislation, instead they sought ways to circumvent the restrictions of coverture through marriage settlements, jointures, and other legal agreements. These agreements set out what financial resources a woman would bring to the marriage and specified the arrangements for a wife's future financial security should she outlive her husband. Many families went further, providing a separate income for a married woman through the establishment of a trust that provided the wife with a source of income during the marriage. Cuthbert Harrison did just this before the marriage of his daughter Lenox to Lyon Pilkington in 1698. He set up a trust that gave his daughter an income separate from Lyon.[19] Lenox was fortunate that her father did so, because on her father's death a year later Lyon claimed all of Lenox's inheritance, as was his legal right under coverture, and then abandoned her leaving her with only the income from the trust set up before the marriage. In her case, at least she had the income from the trust to support her; many other women in similar situations found themselves destitute. For their part, many husbands were often unhappy about these separate trusts, arguing that this arrangement undermined their authority in the household. Thornton Cage complained that his mother-in-law made a separate trust for his wife, which she refused to share with him. He accused her of using this income to live in London among a disreputable crowd, including her cousin, whom he claimed was her lover as well.[20]

Women and their families also used the complex legal system of England itself, with its various jurisdictions, courts, and particular practices, in an attempt to circumvent the worst repercussions of coverture and often resorted to the courts of equity to air grievances that could not be admitted in the common law courts. Judges in the courts of equity showed a willingness to consider cases involving married women because of cultural concepts of fairness.[21] These courts often recognized the gross inequity and abuse that occurred within some marriages. However, access to the courts of equity was restricted. Women could lodge a suit only if they had the money to pay the court fees and a man who would bring the suit to the court for them. (Technically the judgment would be for or against the man who entered the suit, not the woman for whom the suit was brought.) Tobias Cage complained that an unnamed male friend of his wife's interfered in his marriage by starting a law suit against him on her behalf.[22] Sir Benjamin Tickbourne sued Robert Garth for his daughter, Grace.[23] A male relative of Anne Lloyd filed a suit for her after her husband, Humphrey, "assaulted, beat and wounded [her] moste pyttyfully." She told the court that "for saufegarde of her life" she had to "departe away from him" without any money for herself or her child, whom she also carried away with her.[24] In this unusual case the court restored to Anne all the property she brought to the marriage and it allowed her to retain all the income from her property in her own hands. She was also allowed to live separately from Humphrey. This favorable outcome for Anne was probably influenced by the constant contempt Humphrey showed the court, which eventually landed him in the Fleet Prison.

Women could also seek help from the ecclesiastical or church courts. Here wives could bring a complaint against their husbands in their own name. This was because these courts dealt with matters related to moral transgressions, and thus the interests of individuals within a marriage were recognized. Matters that came to these courts included accusations of marital cruelty, adultery, and questions regarding the validity of a marriage. The courts were concerned about restoring the moral health of individuals and the reestablishment of social harmony. This sometimes meant allowing a couple to live apart, with the husband providing financial assistance to the wife (though he was not required to return any of her property to her). The Countess of Anglesey brought to the church courts her accusations of being beaten on the breast and thrown down the stairs and was awarded a separate financial maintenance, along with the right to live away from her husband. Angela Cottington complained that her husband, Charles, abandoned her after their marriage in Italy, pretending no marriage had taken place. The church courts agreed the marriage was valid, awarded Angela alimony of £300 per year, and again gave her permission to live apart from her husband.[25] Mary Hampson brought her complaints against Robert Hampson to the church courts and was also allowed to live separately from him, along with being awarded a maintenance of £100 per year. Unfortunately, though the church courts found in Mary's favor, by 1670 they had very little power to enforce their decisions. Many women often had great difficulty collecting their alimony and thus suffered severe financial hardship. In addition a separation could be disastrous for a woman's social standing. Many women in this situation found themselves ostracized from their social networks, adding emotional hardship to their often precarious financial situation. Even worse, children remained with the husband in most of these cases, and a woman was often denied access to them.

The only exception in common law to the legal restrictions of coverture was related to criminal offenses committed by the husband or the wife. The lawyer Robert Brook explained in his treatise on coverture that in the case of criminal behavior and imprisonment of the husband, the property a woman brought to the marriage should not be seized, because, as he put it, "the husband and wife are not one person" and thus she could not be forced to endure the same penalties as her husband.[26] Though of course the seizure of the husband's property, as was usual on a criminal conviction, would certainly create a hardship for most women, especially if they had brought money rather than property to the marriage. In addition, all of a woman's contributions to the household of a financial or practical nature would be lost to the state on her husband's conviction. A husband could also be financially at a loss if his wife was convicted of a criminal offense. In a case where the wife was convicted of a criminal offense, the practice of folding all of the wife's money and moveable property into the household upon marriage would insulate the husband much more; all he stood to lose was any land she held in her own name, that is, freehold land. And yet, despite the practical nature of Brook's observation that "the husband and wife are not one person," he, and society more generally, refused to acknowledge the suffering of women whose livelihoods and even physical safety were often endangered by the restrictions of coverture as practiced in the period.

Women who were abandoned by their husbands, or forced to flee because of abuse, were confronted by the often shocking reality that under coverture their options for redress remained very limited. Their ability to protect themselves and their property was dependent on the financial resources they could draw on, and the support they could expect from their families and friends. It also depended on their willingness to risk the social ostracism and condemnation visited upon most women who separated from their husbands. Thus separation was often the last resort of the abused or abandoned wife. Instead, many women consulted popular advice books of the time. These books set out for women appropriate behavior within marriage, including how to deal with an abusive spouse.[27] The advice in these books was not particularly encouraging in this regard. John Dod and Richard Cleaver's *A Godly form of Householde Government* (1612) and William Gouge's *Of Domesticall Duties* (1622) counseled obedience and patience. Thomas Bentley in his *Fifth Lamp of Virginitie* (1582) suggested prayer rather than action. He even provided a specific prayer for women faced with "a froward and bitter husband" for the purpose of avoiding "the mischiefe of divorcement and separation:"

> O Most wise and provident God . . . if it be thy good pleasure with frowardnes, bitternes, and unkindnesse, yea, the hatred and disdaine of my husband, thus to correct me for my fault, I most hartilie thanke thee for it. And I beseech thee, so to order me in all things in thy great mercie, that I never murmur or grudge impatientlie against thee for the same, nor doo anie thing either against thee or my husband . . . but deere God, give mee perfect patience, I beseech thee; and that I for my part may quietlie beare the frailtie, infirmities and faults of my husband, with more patience, mildnesse and modestie, than hitherto I have.[28]

Few women in abusive marriages were able to apply this advice in the long run, though there is much evidence to suggest that many were desperate to find a solution to violence and deprivation that would allow them to live peaceably with their husbands. For, as Mary Hampson's story shows, separation had severe social and financial costs, especially for women. The astrologer-physician Richard Napier treated more than a hundred women for depression brought on by marital abuse between 1598 and 1602. In the 1670s Peter Banks sold remedies to cure cruel husbands. One desperate wife paid him ten shillings and two new shirts for the chance of one year's happiness.[29] However, most women, finding prayer and supernatural cures ineffective, sought the help of family, friends, neighbors, respected members of their community or social group, and even strangers. These individuals, in their turn, accepted that they had a responsibility to help reestablish marital harmony—or at least to find a way to help the couple live more "quietly" together.

The Hampson marriage shows evidence of heavy social intervention on the part of a surprisingly large and diverse number of people. The many documents connected with this marriage reveal the participation in their marital problems of more than 170 individuals. In the early years of the Hampson marriage, the foremost were Mary's mother, Elizabeth Wingfield, and her uncle, John Whalley. Elizabeth often provided financial support, especially during periods when Robert Hampson would not arrange housing or maintenance for Mary. Elizabeth also attempted to convince Mary to leave Robert and live with her, a course that Mary recognized would be socially devastating. John Whalley withheld property promised to the couple in an attempt to force Robert into making reasonable financial arrangements for Mary; Whalley later left the property to Mary and her heirs in his will. This had the effect of securing the income from the property for Mary once Robert died, though Robert had full use of the income during his life. Mary also had a powerful ally in Mary Aubrey Montagu,[30] the wife of William Montagu, a judge and politician, and the second son of Edward 1st Baron Montagu. Mary Montagu brokered reconciliations and constantly supported Mary Hampson both emotionally and practically. She is most likely the friend who encouraged Mary to publish the story of her marriage.

Others who helped Mary, often at great risk to themselves, include John Fiennes, the son of William Fiennes, Viscount Saye and Sele. John was beaten on one occasion when he went to collect Mary's alimony. Another ally, Mary's maid, Katherine Brown, was sent to prison for helping Mary sell some household objects after Robert abandoned Mary. Robert had Katherine charged with theft because under coverture all the possessions in the house were his. Other assistance came from a Mistress Guin, who gave Mary shelter after Robert threatened her with a pistol. The next day she walked Mary back to Robert's chambers and demanded an explanation from him. Mary also wrote of an incident where Robert's clerk threw her into the street and called her a madwoman to incite the crowd. An unknown woman waded into the mob and pulled her to safety.

This support by family, friends, and even strangers is also shown in the autobiography of another abused wife, Margaret Cunningham. In 1608 she wrote an account of her disastrous marriage in order to justify her separation from her husband, though she chose to circulate the manuscript among friends rather than publish it in the press. Margaret's story differs in its particular details from Mary Hampson's, but not in the desperation of her situation. Her husband, Sir James Hamilton, often lived with his mistress while Margaret was left pregnant, in poverty, and at times homeless. Margaret recounts at one point that:

> My husband conceved a great anger against me, (he being in fancie with Jean Boyd) and he would not come in to the house I was in. I tooke sickness and lay bed fast six week. I requested my Lady mother to deal with him [James] . . . being altogether destitute . . . my Lady mother sent my sister Mrs Susanna to Evandale to me, and desired me to come with her.

Margaret's marriage never improved. Her autobiography recounts the futile efforts of her parents, her sister, and even her husband's parents to try to convince James Hamilton to fulfill his marital obligations. All of these attempts provided only a temporary reprieve, and often she had to look for help from servants and the wider community. On one terrible night, she was thrown out of her house heavily pregnant, and despite being ordered by James to leave her, a servant and his wife helped Margaret find shelter at a minister's house.[31]

Unfortunately, in the cases of both Mary Hampson and Margaret Cunningham, these interventions were ineffective in producing anything but a short reprieve in the abuse. In the final conflict before her separation, Mary was barred from her house by Robert's armed friends. Expelled from her home without even a change of clothing, her only option was to appeal to the church or ecclesiastical courts to reestablish her conjugal right to financial support from her husband. Recourse to the legal system was generally a last resort for women (and men) because of social disapproval and loss of reputation. But when the differences between a couple were truly irreconcilable, a suit in an ecclesiastical court often followed. These courts had jurisdiction over marital misconduct because refusal to fulfill one's marital obligations was generally considered a moral crime. The church courts could demand a couple return to cohabitation or they could grant a legal separation—a separation from bed and board (*a mensa et thoro*). This allowed married couples to live apart legally.

A separation of this kind did not permit the remarriage of either individual; nor did it absolve the husband of financial responsibility for maintaining his wife—except in cases where it could be proved that the wife had committed adultery or felonious acts. A separation also did not require the return of property or money brought to the marriage by the wife. Mary Hampson was successful in securing a separation but was less successful in collecting the alimony that was agreed, or as she bitterly complained, "There is no penalty against Mr. Hampson but excommunication . . . and I have not bread to live on." The story of her decades-long attempts to collect her alimony is retold in both the autobiographical pamphlet presented here and the many legal documents connected to her case, discussed in the following chapters.

By the early 1680s, Mary Hampson had exhausted all the usual and limited avenues of redress open to her. Despite the intervention of high-status individuals such as John Fiennes and Mary and William Montagu, Robert Hampson continued to refuse to pay the alimony he had agreed to during the High Court of Delegates case in 1670. This was a court that heard appeals against judgments from other courts, including the ecclesiastical. Robert had appealed to this court after the Court of Arches decision favored Mary and required him to fulfill his marital responsibility of supporting her. The High Court of Delegates had no permanent judges. Instead, a commission of men called judges or delegates was set up for each case. By the end of the seventeenth century this commission was generally made up of civilians and common law lawyers. The typical commission had three commissioners; the commission set up to hear Robert Hampson's appeal was unusual in that it was made up of twelve delegates. Mary's relationship with her particular commission of delegates was quite long, lasting for more than fifteen years. This commission, which in the end was composed of only two men, Thomas Exton and Thomas Pinfold (the other judges having died), was still hearing pleas related to the case as late as 1684 because of Robert's continued refusal to pay Mary the agreed maintenance of £100 per year.

This intransigence on Robert's part is difficult to explain, though it appears by the mid-1660s he had given up any attempt to salvage his reputation in the wider gentry community. Instead he isolated himself within the Inner Temple.[32] It seems that his marital problems did not interfere with his legal work and his promotion within the legal community. On the contrary, he was appointed as a Sergeant of Law in 1680.[33] This was a prestigious appointment that recognized his skill in law and his professional reputation. The appointment also indicates that Mary's well-placed friends, such as the Fiennes and Montagus, were not willing to interfere with Robert's professional advancement, despite what they may have thought about his reprehensible behavior toward his wife.

During this time Robert Hampson also negotiated an advantageous marriage for their daughter Elizabeth, to Charles Bill. The two men met when Bill was going through legal wrangles of his own with the executor of his father's will. The wedding was held in the Inner Temple church, and it was clearly seen as a triumph for Hampson. It was likely a costly triumph, as legal documents reveal that Bill could be both tenacious and unscrupulous in monetary matters. It is unlikely this marriage would have taken place without Hampson making a hefty financial payment to Bill. The Hampsons' second daughter, Mary, later complained that she lived in poverty, suggesting that Robert used many of his resources to secure Elizabeth's marriage and had nothing left for Mary. Robert was also very busy at this time investing in the rebuilding of the Inner Temple after the Great Fire of London in 1666, and a second fire in the Inner Temple in 1677 that also caused considerable damage.[34] Given his building projects and the marriage of his eldest daughter in the early 1680s, Robert Hampson had little extra cash and violently resented Mary's appeals for alimony.

An added complication was Mary's move to mainland Europe. In the mid-1660s, after a particularly brutal beating by her husband while she was pregnant, Mary went to France for nearly two years on the advice of her doctor.[35] After the couple agreed to the terms of their separation, Mary decided to return to the continent, because, as she explained, she was both afraid of her husband and ashamed by the loss of her reputation. This move provided Robert with ample opportunity to avoid paying Mary any alimony. At one point he stated in a legal document that he believed she was dead (as will be discussed more fully in Chapter Two). Even eyewit-

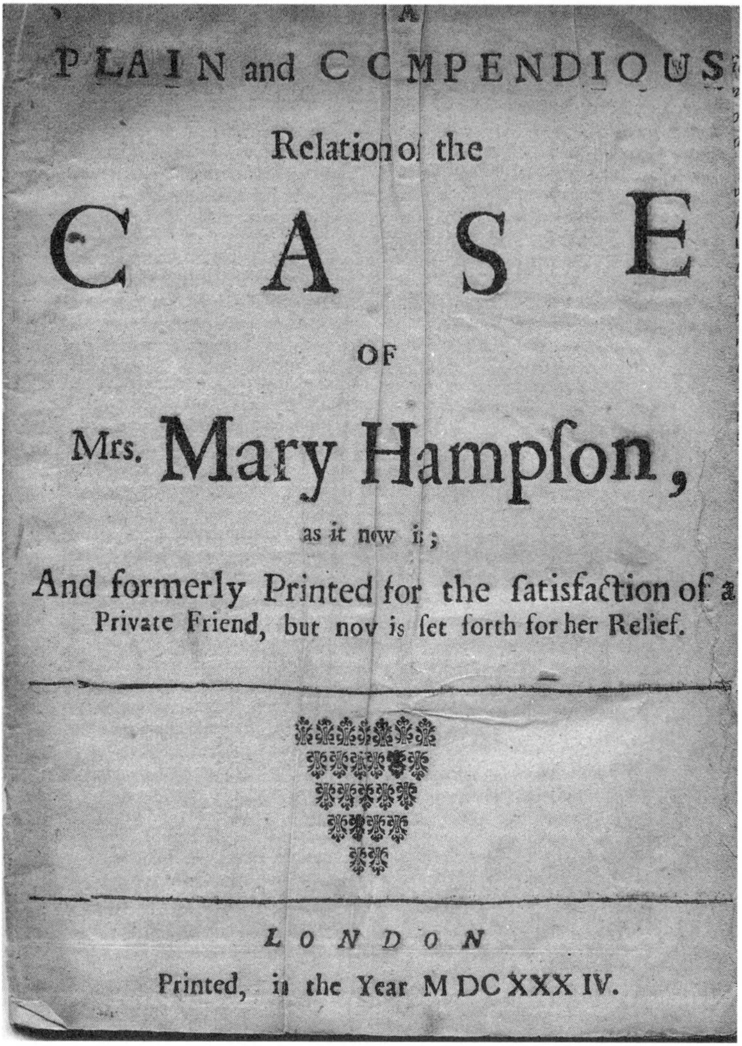

A

PLAIN and COMPENDIOUS

Relation of the

CASE

OF

Mrs. Mary Hampson,

as it now is;

And formerly Printed for the fatisfaction of a
Private Friend, but now is fet forth for her Relief.

LONDON

Printed, in the Year M DC XXX IV.

FIGURE 2. Title page, (London, 1684). Author's collection.

ness accounts of his own relatives and other gentry did not convince Robert that his wife was alive. It was at this juncture, after several attempts to secure her alimony, that Mary decided to publish her mistreatment more broadly in the form of the autobiographical pamphlet.

In October 1680 Mary wrote to the lawyer, and later ambassador and politician, Sir William Trumbull: "I think it will be necessary for me to put the case, as it is betwixt Mr. Hampson and myself, in print in all countries that the world may know the true reasons of our difference."[36] Interestingly, in this letter she first writes "in writing" but crosses this out and replaces it with the phrase "in print." At this point it is evident she views putting her story in print as a last resort or extreme measure. However, shortly after this letter she must have begun writing her story in earnest.

The title page of her pamphlet proclaims it was written "for the satisfaction of a private friend, but now is set forth [or published] for her relief." This sort of address, which excused the act of writing and invoked the presence of a high-status individual, was not unusual at the time, and it was especially common in works published by women. Mary's insistence that the publication was done because of her extreme need was intended to secure the sympathy of the reading public, making them receptive to the story that followed. The opening address also explains Mary's decision to publish, and it notes that she prepared an earlier version of the story that was destroyed. According to information Mary shares later in the story, the 1684 edition published in London was not the first edition of her story. This first edition, she tells the reader, was published by the printer Henry Goddeaus in Rotterdam in 1682 or 1683. And here we meet one of the oddest and most dangerous individuals in her story: the traitor, spy, and informer Edmund Everard. He was a notorious double agent who figured in the Popish Plot of 1678,[37] though the exact nature of his role remains unclear. In 1682 he was in the Netherlands informing on the English living there. Mary claims that Everard burnt the Rotterdam edition of her pamphlet on Robert Hampson's instructions.

The destruction of her first print run, rather than discouraging Mary, appears to have made her more determined than ever to present her side of the story to the public. She updated the account, and in 1684 it appeared in print at the London booksellers. The name of the printer does not appear on the title page. This does not mean the publication was in any way clandestine. Projects funded by the author were often printed without the printer's name and instead with only the phrase "Printed in the year" or simply "Printed." Mary makes it clear that she funded the printing of this pamphlet. It is likely that the printer was Benjamin Harris, an associate of Henry Goddeaus, the Rotterdam publisher who printed the earlier pamphlet. The size of the print run again cannot be known. Typically a first commercial print run would be about two hundred copies. However, despite Mary's insistence on the cover page that the publication was for her "relief" or to provide her with some income, it is unlikely that her pamphlet was produced on a commercial scale, and there may have been far fewer than two hundred copies printed, though unusually for this type of pamphlet a second printing followed the first with only minor additions at the end of the pamphlet.

Today only three of Mary's pamphlets are known to survive. Such pamphlets were cheap, and they were viewed more as entertainment than as literary investments, much like newspapers or magazines today. After they were read, they were often reused for wrapping, lining shelves or baking tins, or in other ways not conducive to a high rate of survival. Also, given Mary's compromised social status, and the sensational nature of the story, few readers would have thought to save her work for posterity. The survival of even three copies is thus rather remarkable and clearly accidental.[38]

The publication itself is unique in many ways. There was a taste for publishing and reading about marital disharmony in the later seventeenth century, but Mary's story is by far the longest and most complex of those that survive. Much of what can be termed "marital problem" publications were short pieces, often printed on one broadsheet, similar to one page of newspaper print. Others printed their stories in short pamphlets of two to four pages. Some of these are *The case of Angela Margarita Cottington* (1680); *The case between Thornton Cage and his wife* (1684); and

The case of Mary, Dutchess of Norfolk (1700). These publications are generally summary reports of court cases, though Cage's four-page pamphlet is told as a first-person narrative.

Unlike the shorter pamphlets or broadsheets, Mary Hampson's book is ten pages of closely printed text, thirteen thousand words long. And unlike the shorter pieces, it is a fully developed autobiographical narrative that provides extensive context and detail. The only other surviving pamphlet published in this genre that is as detailed and developed as Mary Hampson's is a narrative written by Tobias Cage: *A letter to a person of quality, occasioned by a printed libel entitled, "The cause of the difference between Tobias Cage esquire, and Mary his wife stated by the said Mary in a letter to a gentleman, for her own vindication"* (1678). It may be that this publication suggested to Mary the possibility of seeking redress through the publication of her own story. And even though we cannot know if she saw Cage's pamphlet, there is one interesting connection between the two stories. The Inner Temple lawyer Richard Powell and his wife appear in both stories as siding with the abusive spouses—Robert in Mary's case and Mary Cage in Tobias Cage's story.

If Mary did read this publication, she should have paid closer attention to one phrase on Cage's title page: "occasioned by a printed libel." Cage's pamphlet was a response to his wife's printed accusations of marital cruelty, where she accused Cage of attempting to stab her and cut her throat and of withholding her money from her.[39] Robert Hampson, like Tobias Cage, was quick to respond to Mary's printed accusations. A pamphlet called *A Relation of the design of Mrs. Hampson to poison or stab her husband* appeared in 1685.[40] This pamphlet refers to incidents that are found in the court depositions and Everard's pamphlet *The Depositions and Examinations of Mr. Edmund Everard . . . Concerning the Horrid Popish Plot* (1679) and will be discussed in more detail in Chapter Two. Robert Hampson's pamphlet was likely the reason Mary published a second edition of her own pamphlet. Her second edition was unusual in publications of this sort, as they were generally one-off publications. This second edition contains only one short, but telling, addition to the text of the first pamphlet, found on the

Mrs. Hampsons
C A S E.

Mr. *Ampson* is a younger Son of Sr. *Thomas Hampson*, who was Master of the *Statute Office*, and one of the undertakers, or adventurers in the draining of *Fenlands*.

Mr. *Hampson* did before the death of his Father, make a request unto him, that he might have the refusal of the *Fenlands*
after his death, which was granted ; and after his death Mr.
Hampson did buy the *Fenlands* of his Brothers and Sisters, and
did ingage to them by Recognisance, all the Estate he had for their security ; after
this, his business was a Wife, he had made his Addresses to many , but I suppose their
friends were too wise to be deceived, but by sad misfortune to me, he came to *Chat-
tres* in the *Isle* of *Ilee*, to look after his *Fenlands*, and lay at a Ministers house, an acquaintance of my Mothers, which Minister brought him to see me with the Reputation
of a man of a very considerable Estate, his Fathers only Executor. Mr. *Hampson* told
my Mother and Uncle, that his Father left nothing to Sr. *Thomas* his Brother, but
what he could not give to him, and that the very goods in *Taplow*-House was his, and
many other Stories to them and me, which we was so innocent to believe ; he had got
in a short time so much into my Mothers and Uncles favour, that they would not admit of no other person to speak to me but him, so things were agreed upon, & I had a
Joynture made me of that Estate which was ingaged to his Brothers and Sisters, and
was married to him, he brought me up to *London*, to his house in *Holbourn* ; two of
his Sisters were with him some time, and Mr. *Turner* and his Family : his Sisters were
so civil as not to trouble him for their monys, untill I was brought to bed, and up a-
gain ; then the dispute betwixt Mr. *Hampson* and his Sisters was so hot in his Study
one Night, that the out-cry came to me, then Mr. *Hampson* told me he had no way to
keep himself out of Prison, and that he was ruined if I did not consent to the sale of
my Joynture : the trouble I saw Mr. *Hampson* in, caused me o forget my own safety,
so that I went with him to my *Lord Chief Justice*, but so soon as he knew I was under
age, he would not give Audience, but returned to his inner Chamber ; I had not then
the judgment to discern that he was my friend in so doing , but took it for a slight,
which troubled me more than if I had releas'd my Joynture : so much a Child I was,
and

FIGURE 3. *A Plain and Compendious Relation of the Case of Mrs. Mary Hampson*, page 1.
Author's collection.

final printed page. Here Mary places a quotation from the 1671 agreement that came out of the High Court of Delegates in which Robert Hampson agreed to pay alimony and was under the threat of excommunication should he not comply. Mary hoped her readers would realize that such an agreement would not have been entered into by Robert had he been able to prove Mary guilty of attempted murder. She could realistically expect her readers to understand that if the court believed she had plotted murder, Robert would have been awarded a separation with no financial obligations to Mary. Mary concludes this quotation of their agreement by adding the name of the registrar of the High Court of Delegates, Thomas Oughton, in order to assert the validity of the agreement.[41]

Mary Hampson's story may have come from financial need. But what fueled her determination to print her tribulations was her deep sense of injustice. She published this account of her marriage in order to speak out against a man who she believed had robbed her of her innocence, her children, her mother, her money, her social position, and her dignity. Mary's autobiography is a chilling account not only of one husband's cruelty but also of the repercussions of a legal system that forced a wife to be "covered" by her husband and denied effective legal redress for wrongs done to her.

Mary writes of her trials with great passion and energy and reveals her indomitable spirit through the course of her story. In her pamphlet *A Plain and Compendious Relation of the Case of Mrs. Mary Hampson*, Mary speaks in her own voice and exercises her authority in relating the events of her life. This autobiography was born out of Mary's suffering, but it also emerged from other stories about the marriage told in thirty-four legal documents, seven letters, one monument inscription, and one other surviving pamphlet. In these, Mary's struggles appear at times less heroic, but perhaps more human. The raw material from which Mary shaped her own printed story can be found in them. Here we see her troubled relationships with her mother, husband, and children in greater detail than in her 1684 printed story. These relationships are explored in the chapters that follow Mary's printed autobiography presented here. In these chapters, Mary's repression or simplification of events and circumstances provides intriguing information about how she saw herself, and also the role cultural expectations played in how she presents and discusses the events of her life in her pamphlet. This exploration of Mary's story, through the many documents connected to it, also reveals how the legal restrictions found in seventeenth-century marriages had profound consequences not only for the couple caught up in a disastrous marriage but also for the people connected with the marriage. These could include the parents and relatives who instigated the marriage and the children resulting from it, along with the wider familial and social circles connected to the couple.

Leo Tolstoy opens his novel *Anna Karenina* with the famous line "Happy families are all alike; every unhappy family is unhappy in its own way." Had he dipped into the legal depositions and the popular press of seventeenth-century England, he might have revised this statement to include the acknowledgment that even though every unhappy marriage certainly was unique, how this unhappiness was expressed, the strategies employed by those involved, and finally the social structures that contributed to unhappy marriages were often quite similar, as can be seen in the case of Mrs. Mary Hampson.

A

PLAIN and COMPENDIOUS

Relation of the

CASE

OF

Mrs. Mary Hampson

as it now is

And formerly Printed for the satisfaction of a
Private Friend but now is set forth for her Relief.

LONDON 1684

The spelling of the original document has been retained. Capitalization and punctuation
have been modernized.

My Dear Friend:

Did I not know you to be of that little number who have compassion upon the oppressed, although their own simplicity and imprudence may have been partly the cause, by giving occasion to the wicked contrivers to work their ends, otherwise I should not have consented to give you the Relation, of the contrivances of Mr. Hampson, which hath brought me now under so great oppression. For I believe the world will say, she is well rewarded. Why was she so simple? I having found in this age, an honest simplicity is so out of fashion, that I may fear to be laughed to scorn for my too good nature to Mr. Hampson, rather than hope for compassion from the generality. I must also in my Relation acuse my mother and uncle to have been too easie of belief, and little care in the matching of me. But I question not but that which doth excuse them to me, will do so to you. They were so honest and just dealers, and truly good that they took Mr. Hampson's bare word as to his estate, and believed his great protestations which he made unto them that there was no engagement upon it. This plaine simple way of dealing will seem strange to the world. But I know that the unheard of ingratitude, and the continual practices of falsities, and cruelties, which Mr. Hampson used to save his credit in the world, and ruine mine, will give you horrour. Had he not made away or caused to be made away my mother's will? By which to avoid Mr. Hampson's coming to her estate, she gave it in trust to Sir Nicholas Pedly of Huntington[1] and Mr. Pont[2] of the same town. And sometime after her death finding he could not prevail with me to give him my bonds,[3] he made a false non cupitive will,[4] and got it witnessed by a man to whom he owed monyes, and a maid servant of no credit.[5] They never were examined nor as I believe sworn. With this pretended will he went into the country, and there received monys, made bonds in his name, sold my houses,[6] and when he came to town[7] turned me out of the house where I lived,[8] took from me a hundred & fifty pounds in gold my mother had given me upon her death-bed, all my clothes and jewels to the value of much more. But my dear friend, all this I could have supported had the world known the true cause of Mr. Hampson's violence. You will find in all my relation that my friends and I have wanted the wisdom of the world, and that Mr. Hampson, hath wanted Christianity in the whole matter. As to the manner how Mr. Hampson appeared a man of an estate to the world, (which deceived my friends) I came to know by the letters I took out of his study when I lived with him in the Temple,[9] but he has since got them from me by his craft and falseness of the person with whom I intrusted them: my mother's bonds, the receipt of my portion,[10] many other writings and things of good value. The person with whom I had intrusted them told me his chambers was broke open, and nothing stolen but my box and a red trunck of one of his brothers in law which had H.W. upon it. To colour the matter the said person put in the Gazzette[11] how his door was broke open, and such a box and trunck stolen. The next morning I went with a friend to his chamber, to discourse with him about this robbery. We found him alone and a night-gown on, of the very same stript Indian satin which I had several pieces of in my box. When I saw that, I believed I was betrayed, and not before, for I did not think the said person capable of so base an action. You knowing the person is the reason I do not name him.[12] For it is for your satisfaction only that I write this relation following: how Mr. Hampson got me, my estate and credit amongst some persons, and by what wayes I am brought unto so sad a condition. For having thus been betrayed out of Mr. Hampson's letters, his fathers, brothers, and sisters letters when they were at difference with him for their monys, which my joynture was pre-engaged for,[13] my mother's and uncles's letters I want, to be so strong in my evidence it may be to convince such persons as do not know me, how highly wronged I have been, and am. But I hope you will be fully perswaded, that I have not merrited the disgrace I suffer under. And if I cannot pretend to your esteem, because of so great want of judgment which you will find me guilty of, by my own confession, I flatter myself with the hopes of a true compassion from you, which will be a very great consolation to

Madam,

your friend,

And most humble

servant

Mary Hampson.

Mrs. Hampson's
C A S E

Mr. Hampson is a younger son of Sir Thomas Hampson, who was Master of the Statute Office, and one of the undertakers, or adventurers in the draining of the fenlands.

Mr. Hampson did before the death of his father, make a request unto him, that he might have the refusal of the fenlands after his death, which was granted. And after his death Mr. Hampson did buy the fenlands of his brothers and sisters,[14] and did ingage to them by recognisance of all the estate he had for their security; after this, his business was a wife. He had made his addresses to many, but I suppose their friends were too wise to be deceived but by sad misfortune to me, he came to Chatres in the Isle of Ilee,[15] to look after his fenlands, and lay at a ministers house, an acquaintance of my mothers, which minister brought him to see me with the reputation of a man of very considerable estate, his father's only executor. Mr. Hampson told my mother and uncle, that his father left nothing to Sir Thomas his brother, but what he could not give to him, and that the very goods in Taplow-House was his, and many other stories to them and me, which we was so innocent to believe.[16] He had got in a short time so much into my mothers and uncle's favour, that they would not admit of no other person to speak to me but him, so things were agreed upon, & I had a joynture made me of that estate which was ingaged to his brothers and sisters, and was married to him. He brought me up to London, to his house in Holbourn. Two of his sisters were with him some time,[17] and Mr. Turner and his family. His sisters were so civil as not to trouble him for their monys,[18] untill I was brought to bed, and

up again.[19] Then the dispute betweext Mr. Hampson and his sisters was
so hot in his study one night, that the out-cry came to me. Then Mr.
Hampson told me he had no way to keep himself out of prison, and that
he was ruined if I did not consent to the sale of my joynture. The trouble
I saw Mr. Hampson in, caused me to forget my own safety,[20] so that I
went with him to my Lord Chief Justice.[21] But so soon as he knew I was
under age, he would not give audience, but returned to his inner chamber.
I had not then the judgment to discern that he was my friend in so doing,
but took it for a slight, which troubled me more than if I had released my
joynture. So much a child I was and I remember my Lord said to me, go
home poor child. After this, Mr. Hampson brought me to one Mr. Hatch
a merchant, who told me that if I would give him a promise under my
hand, to release when I should come of age, he would buy the land and
pay the moneys down, so that Mr. Hampson would be soon out of trouble. And God knows I did do it with joy, not being capable to imagine
that Mr. Hampson did design my ruin. And I did leave a fine when I
came of age.[22] My uncle, which was then a live, hearing what I had done,
wrote to Mr. Hampson, that if he did not make me a new settlement of
a joynture, he would not give me the estate he promised.[23] Upon this
threatening, Mr. Hampson made me a joynture of fenlands, and a house
in Holbourn which was in my first joynture. The feoffees[24] he named in
the deed were one Mr. Henry Poulton[25] that had married a cozen ger-
man[26] of his, and the other a friend, and one unto who Mr. Hampson
owed moneys, as I have reason to believe. His name was Hollman.
Mr. Hampson gave me the writings, and I kept them till such time as he
took them by force from me, as I shall give you an account hereafter.
Mr. Hampson let his house where we lived, to Sir John Holland,[27] and
put me into lodgings, which seemed very strange to me, and did go besides to the circuit many times into the country,[28] and left me but a small
matter to keep me. He told me he went into Norfolk, about the steward-
ship of the honour of Clare.[29] And the last time I was with child[30] a little
before he went, as he said, unto Norfolk, being in the bed with him, I
desired him to let me know how his affairs were in the world, and that he

would not always make me a stranger to his concern as he had done. I did alledge to him the great surprize and trouble I had when I was with child the time before.[31] Which was, that a day or two after he was gone out of town, I received an order from the house of Lords, that Mr. Hampson was to bring in the books that belonged to the Statute Office by Thursday, this was on the Tuesday, or otherwise four Sergeants of Arms were to be sent to take him, a thousand pounds fine, and six months imprisonment, with the House of Lords displeasure.[32] Then I came to know that Mr. Hampson had bought his brothers and sisters part in the books, and pretended that he should make a great profit of them. But they were delivered to Mr. May, then Master of the Statute Office,[33] as I declare to you, by orders from the house of Lords. Mr. Hampson had, as I knew since, borrowed two hundred pounds of Mr. Richard Edward of the Temple not long before to pay his brothers and sisters part in them. This I was speaking to him of, which he was very angry at, and said I reproached him, and did strike me upon the brest which grew very bad.[34] He went out of town, and left me in a sad and weak condition with very little money. I had Doctor Hinton[35] and Doctor Nurses[36] advice. They durst not tamper with me because I was with child. I lay in a very weak and dangerous condition at Mrs. Hermittage's house in Richmond. And when by the great mercy of God I was recovered in part by the means of a woman in Richmond, I came to town. My mother supplyed my wants in all things, for I did not so much as hear from Mr. Hampson untill that night I was delivered. The indisposition of my body joyned to the grief I suffered to finde by all Mr. Hampson's actions that he had not any kindness for me, brought me to a very languishing and weak condition. When I was out of child-bed some three or four months finding I recovered my strength very slowly, I consulted Doctor Nurses, who was physician to most of my relations, and had known me from a child. He would give me no physick[37] but told me my father and most of the Wingfields died of consumptions;[38] and that his only advice to me was to go to Montpellier or some part of France where the air was best. When I proposed this to Mr. Hampson he was very well pleased I should go, provided I cost him but little. He would not be perswaded to give me more than thirty pounds for six months. I accepted of that, knowing I could not want whilst my mother lived, and I had also five hundred pounds in jewels of hers, which I did intend to take with me. About a week before I was to go, Mr. Hampson one morning told me, he hoped I would now believe he had a kindness for me, being he had consented for my health to let me go unto France, and that he would imploy the six months I should be absent about his business of the Honor of Clare. But he would have me before I went to grant him one thing he would desire of me, before he told me what it was, which I refused. Then he told me it was that I should give my consent to sell the house in Holbourn which was part of my joynture, which I absolutely refused, at which he was very angry. About a week after, when I was prepared to go, Mr. Hampson superscribed[39] my trunck to whom he thought good at Dover, and the morning I was to take my journey, he brought according to his word thirty pounds. But withal told me he would have me leave with him the writings of my joynture and my mother's jewels. When I saw him in a violent passion for them, I told him they were in my trunck he sent to Dover. Then he said no more, but took his leave of me. But when I came to Dover my truncks was stoped, but not my person. But the man who received Mr. Hampson's order to seize my trunck did give me counsel to return and speak with Mr. Hampson. I was perswaded to come to London, but was so much affraid that Mr. Hampson would by violent usage make me consent to what he desired concerning my joynture, that I went for Rye,[40] and there stayed some days. After which I went for France. God was so good to me that my jewels were about me and my maid, but the deed of my joynture he got. So soon as he had it to excuse himself, he reported I was run away from him.[41] When I had been in France about two months, my uncle which had settled an estate upon me and such heirs as I pleased, dyed, and I not being in England, Mr. Hampson got it by his ordinary practice into his possession. A little time after God was pleased to visit England with the sickness,[42] so that I thought it not reasonable for me to come unto an infected air, unless it had been necessary for the preservation of him or my children, and so I writ to him. He would not hear any reason from me, nor send me any moneys. But at the time when the news came to the Embassador, that there dyed twelve thousand a week in London, and that Dover was sorely infected; then Mr. Hampson writ to me to come over, or he would never own me, but cast me off. I was very much troubled at his railing letters, and did resolve to venture to go to England, rather than live in so much want and trouble. But meeting with one doctor Noding at Chalenton,[43] a French physician which spoke very good English, and did practice amongst the English, this man did assure me, that going out of a pure air into an infected I should be in greater danger than those that were in England, and that there were some gentlemen who ventured to go home, so soon as they came to Dover dyed of the sickness. This news stopped my journey. Upon consideration I thought it not just to venture my life to go to a man that valued not mine. Then I redoubled my supplications for money to supply my wants, letting him know, that was he in my place, and I in his, my fervent and earnest desires should be for him to keep in safety, did it cost me all I had, or could pretend too in this world. I had no answer, but cruel threatnings in railing letters. I could not send to my mother, not knowing what part of England she was retired, and she could not send to me but by Mr. Hampson, who did pretend to her, he knew not in what part of France I was. She then made her will, and gave her estate to her nephew, Mr. Thomas Walley, as feoffee in trust[44] for me, to avoid Mr. Hampsons being master of it. As she shewed me, so soon as I by God's great mercy got to England. And whilst I was in France, I must have starved or begged but for her jewels. I sold a rose of diamonds to Doctor Noding, I sold my necklace to Mr. Alvares for a thousand guelders. It was worth much more, but in the want I was in, I took what he offered me being in trouble, and ashamed to let my wants be known to persons of quality. I sold diamond rings and other things to Mr. Godar a jeweller in Paris. When the sickness was well abated, my mother by continual and great inquiry amongst those banquires[45] that had correspondence in France, did by the care of Mr. John Cook, a merchant, come to hear where I was lodged in Paris. So soon as my mother knew, she wrote a very tender letter to me, and sent with it a letter of exchange, the banquires name was Burr, and he was so civil as to come himself and bring me my mother's letter, and the moneys she had ordered. My joy was not small, to hear that the Lord was pleased to spare her life in such a time of danger, and that there was no change in her affection towards me, for Mr. Hampson had, (to augment my sorrow,) informed me that she was much offended that I would not come over. I found by her letter, all that was false, and stayed in France untill I could come with safety home. And when I was safe in England I went to my mother. She perswaded me to live with her, telling me she had to maintain me, and that I should let him go with what he had, and that her estate should be a future maintenance for me. This was good advice, but I was so trouble that Mr. Hampson had reported that I went away from him. I thought I had wrong enough to have the deed my joynture taken by force out of my custody, and nothing from him whilst I lived in France, and could not with moderation suffer that horrid untruth he had put forth, to excuse his false and unchristian actions and cruel usage of me. My mother brought me to London, and I against her will went to him at the Temple. When he saw me he laid violent hands upon me, to put me by force out of his chamber.[46] I resisting, he went out and locked me up untill he had dined, and consulted what was best for him to do. He came back and told me he was willing to live with me, if I would sign a paper of articles.[47] The first was that I should say I had gone from him without his consent. I knew not then his design, but knowing it was false I could not do it. Some others there were which were very rediculous. Then he told me he wanted moneys, and I must borrow him five hundred pounds of one Mr. Baker of Windsor, which was a man I had no power with, or of my mother. These were strange demands.[48] The persons commonly of his counsel were the two feoffees named in the joynture, Mr. Poulton and Mr. Holman, and Mr. Edwards[49] did appear with him. When Mr. Hampson saw I would force him to prove that I went from him, which he could not do, he was glad to comply with me for fear I should set fourth his practice. Then he put me to board with an acquaintance of his and Mr. Holmans, and one

morning he brought me a deed, and told me he would be an honest man
to me, and because he was going out of town, he would seal it that day. I
could no longer believe Mr. Hampson, but shewed it to Mr. Sergeant
Maynard,[50] who bid me to tell Mr. Hampson it was worth nothing.
When Mr. Hampson came to seal it, I told him what counsel said. He
replied little in answer, and that day went into the country. I was very ill
used by the woman where he left me, but staid there untill he came back
to town. I desired him to put me somewhere else. He would have me to
live at his chambers in the Temple,[51] which I did. But after I had been
there some time, he would have me give up the right I had in the deed of
joynture he took out of my trunck he stoped when I went to France, for
he had an occasion to sell to a good advantage a parcel of fenlands and
that the persons would not venture to buy without my consent. I told
him I would not consent to any such thing. He said if I would not, I
should not stay in the Temple, nor eat, nor drink, untill I did give my
consent to give up my right in the deed of joynture. The same night he
brought to sup with him his friend, Mr. Powel and his wife,[52] and one
Mr. Shuter, of the Temple.[53] The said Shuter began the discourse for
which they came, and told me that if I was his wife, and denied what he
desired, he would put me into chains and send me to Bedlam,[54] or set me
on my head and make a spread-eagle of me.[55] These and much other un-
sufferable words and carriage I received patiently at my own table, knowing Mr. Hampson's design was to move me to a passion. About twelve a
clock, when those persons were gone I cryed out in my chamber, against
Mr. Hampson for his cruel usage to me. Some persons that passed under
the window heard the words I spoke, and said something in my behalf.[56]
Mr. Hampson at the same instant went and lay with the said Shuter,[57]
and the next morning came to my bed-side, and told me if I would not
arise and be gone I should starve there. For he had given strict order to
my maid, his clark and laundress, not to let me have anything to eat. And
all that day I could get nothing to eat. The next morning Mr. Hampson
came in a rage and bid me to arise and be gone, or the Officers of the
House[58] should come and take me away by force. I knew that if I did go

out of the Temple, he would say I was gone from him, so that I endured very much before I would go. He came to me at twelve a clock, and seeing my maid had brought me some broth to drink, did threaten her. About eleven a clock at night I went into his study to speak with him, hoping his fury was abated. He drew a pistol out of his pocket and set it to my throat saying, that if I would not be gone out of his lodgings he would kill me. (This he hath confessed in his answer in the Spiritual Court, where he stood excommunicated).[59] When I saw that my life was so much in danger, I went at that time of night with my maid into the street, and by good providence got a lodging at one Mr. Guin's at the Temple Gate. The next day was Sunday, and on the Munday morning there came some gentlemen into Mr. Guin's Shop, and told the news, that Mrs. Hampson was run away from her husband. Mrs. Guin did not know me, but thought it might be me, and came up to me. And knowing it was I, she counselled me to go to Mr. Hampson's chambers, and she would go with me, which she did, and asked him if he had turned me out of doors for dishonesty. He answered the said Mrs. Guin: No, it was for my devilish tongue. He rose up and locked his bed-chamber and went out. And towards the evening came home in a more moderate humor, and continued so untill I spoke to him to restore me the writings of my joynture. Then he fell unto the same rage as before, telling me I should starve, or eat his chamber walls if I would not go, and continuing to say the same words the next morning, adding, that if I did not get up presently, the Officers of the House should pull me out of my bed. These words caused me to arise, although I was very much indisposed, and did then tell him he was a dishonest man, and had cheated me. Then he layed violent hands upon me, striking and kicking me so cruelly that I believe he had killed me, had not some persons come in to speak with him. I returned to my bed not being able to do otherwise, and sent for Mr. Serjant Fountain[60] which was my counsel, and to whom Mr. Hampson had promised to make me a new settlement. He was pleased to come; and his presence allayed Mr. Hampson's fury for that time. After this the said Serjant went to my mother, and told her if she would not have me go a begging; and for certain, if it pleased God I out-lived Mr. Hampson, she must settle her estate in feoffees hands for my use. She said she had done so when I was in France. The feoffee was her nephew Thomas Walley, as I have already mentioned before. The Serjant desired she would make a new will, and he would draw it, which he did. And the feoffees then named was: Mr. Nicholas Pedley of Huntington, and Mr. Pont of the same town. Mr. Petet of Bernards Inn,[61] and his brother were witnesses to it. A little after this Mr. Hampson, took me a lodging in St. Martins-Lane, and went unto the country. When he came up again, I told him it was a great trouble for me to be tossed from place to place, and did pray him to take a house. He told me that would be too chargeable, unless I would submit to let lodgings. I did agree to that, and Mr. Hampson hired a house and furnished it, but with very small charge. For the best bed I had was a poor printed paragon,[62] in the dineing room was a suit of ordinary tapestry-hangings which was all the furniture that I had which was creditable. There came several persons to see the house, which liked it, because it was clean and the furniture new, but Mr. Hampson had put so high a price, that none would come to it. And I confess I was very much unacquainted with the way of letting of lodgings, so Mr. Hampson and I had the house to ourselves. My mother was then in London, and then I waited upon her to render her my duty. She would, when she saw me, and what cruel impressions of grief were in my face, and how strangely sorrow had changed me, cry out against Mr. Hampson, and an aunt in law of mine[63] which has perswaded her to marry me with Mr. Hampson, and fall into such violent passions, and said she had no hand in my marriage, and that my aunt had ruined me. It was true in part, for my aunt had a very great esteem of Mr. Hampson, and would not believe but from himself that he had made me a joynture that was pre-engaged by a recognizance. The good woman heartily had asked my pardon, which I had truly granted her, knowing she had done nothing but with a good intention. For this cause I did not wait upon my mother so often as I ought to have done.[64] I sent most days to inquire of her health, but my maid as I knew afterwards, brought to my mother and to me false stories. She was Mr. Hampson's creature, and as I have been informed since a very infamous woman. Her name was Graden. I turned her out of doors in Mr. Hampson's absence. At that time I was not well, & did not go abroad, but was in a parlour below stairs, wherin I heard and saw all persons that come to the door. About four or five days before my mother dyed, one Mr. George Wootten, a kinsman of mine, by trade an uppholster, he asked the maid that opened the door if Mr. Hampson was within, she said no, but her Mistress was. He went away and would not come in to speak with me. I knew he had furnished all my house, and thought he came for moneys. That same afternoon I sent my new maid which was then faithful, to wait upon my mother, and know how she did. The maid brought me word she was not well, and that her maid would not let her speak to my mother. The maid that waited on her, was the daughter of the house where she lay. I then mistrusted that all was not right, and next morning went to my mother and found her in a very weak condition. I kneeled down, she asked me why I had been so long absent. I could not excuse myself but begged her pardon, then she weeped and said, the dissembling cheat hath kept me from my child. It was true, for my mother's passions were become so strong fits of the mother, that he would me forbear to go, for such fits were malignant, and I being a young woman, the consequence was too dangerous.[65] I did not alledge this to my mother, but it was true. She then told me he had told her, I did not desire to see her. I satisfied her to the contrary, and asked her what physician she had had, she said not any. Mr. Hampson came that night to town, and came to my mother's lodgings. She then lay quiet. I was very earnest to have the advice of an able physician, at which Mr. Hampson was angry, telling me she would be well when she had slept, and that she used to be so. I remember that there was a man, an acquaintance of Mr. Hampson's then in chamber, which I never saw before nor since. He did likewise assure me there was no danger of her life. Mr. Hampson forced me to go home with him that night and leave my mother. Which were it now to do, I would die rather than leave a friend, much less a mother, which never failed me but in her conduct, not in her love. The next morning I went against Mr. Hampson's will to my mother. I found

her very sick, and some neighbours about her bed that seemed much surprised, telling me they had inquired the day before, and the landlady and
her daughter told them she was no worse than she used to be. For you
must know my mother had kept the chamber, and commonly her bed for
a long time, so great her discontent was for the loss of my fortunes for
Mr. Hampson was then in a very poor condition. I went the said morning
too for Doctor Willis.[66] When he saw her he told me I came too late. He
ordered her some lozenges. I prevailed with her to put a little in her
mouth but it could not pass. That night the daughter of the house which
was her maid, asked her to whom she would give her gold, moneys, and
plate. She answered as angry at such a demand, "to my child, to whom
should I give it?" These words, and finding nothing but marks of tender
love from her were the cause I did not speak to her of the will, wherein
Sir Nicholas Pedley, and Mr. Pont were feoffees in trust for me, not
doubting but I should find that will after her death. The next day I
brought to her the parson of St. Clements, in which parish she lay sick.
The doctor[67] asked me to receive the sacrament, which I durst not do, by
reason I was not prepared as I desired.[68] That evening Mr. Hampson
came and told me, that the next morning he must go out of town and
gave orders to my mother's maid, daughter of the house where she lay,
that if I was so bold as to meddle with anything that belonged to my
mother after her death, she should oppose it, for that I had no right to
anything that was hers, and that if I did he would turn me a begging
when he came back, with many more threatening words and language
unbecoming a Christian, or honest man, which much augmented my
other troubles. The next day towards the evening, my mother drew near
her end. About two hours before she dyed, there came into her chamber
one Mr. Draper, who lay in the Temple because of his debts. The said
man told me he had authority from my husband to seize upon what
money or goods my mother had in that house. I desired him to retire out
of the chamber and took the keys by force from the maid, and took a
purse of gold, and some silver into my possession. But had so many troubles upon me that I forgot to search amongst the papers for the will. The

groans of my dying mother did so afflict me, that I left the chamber not
being able to support so great trouble without any person about me, but
what endeavored my ruine. In this anguish of spirit I retired into another
chamber and forgot my keys. At the same instant my mother departed
this life. The next morning I caused the trunck in which my mother did
use to keep her writings, to be brought to my house, in which I found
bonds to the value of 2000 pounds but not the will. I ordered that my
mother should be kept in sear-cloths[69] untill Mr. Hampson came to
town. And when he came, he buried her in such a miserable manner as I
was ashamed of, and the same night made a feast and obliged me to be at
the table. The next day he demanded the bonds. I told him they were in a
friends hands that would come very speedly to town. I then asked Serjant
Fountain's advice, who advised me to keep the bonds untill Mr. Hampson
made me a settlement of a joynture. When Mr. Hampson asked me again,
I told him if he would make some provision for me, in case I should outlive him, I was ready to deliver them. Upon this refusal he left me, and
did forbid the baker, brewer and butcher to trust me. In his absence I
wrote (by Serjant Fountain's advice) many letters in which I offered to
refer my case to the Bishop of Canterbury or my Lord Chancellor,[70] if
they would be pleased to take the trouble upon them, or any other indif-
ferent person. He never answered but with high railings and threatnings,
telling me I kept his estate from him. When he saw I would not deliver
the bonds, he set up a pretended nuncupitive will,[71] and got the said Mr.
George Wooton to set his hand to it, which as I have said before, came to
speak with Mr. Hampson when my mother lay sick, and would not come
in and speak with me. Likewise the same maid which had the confidence
to ask my mother who should have what was in the chamber, of gold,
silver and plate and other things to whom she answered my child. This
same maid was subborned, to set her hand to the pretended noncupative
will. The tenour of which is, that Mrs Wingfield gave all she had to her
son in law Mr. Robert Hampson, as was to be seen in the Prerogative
Office.[72] By virtue of this will he went into the country, renewed bonds,
sold my houses, received a great deal of my moneys due upon bonds, the

arrears of my joynture. When he had done this he came up to town, and one day came home with him, his friend Mr. Poulton. He came with a design to turn me out of doors, but at my chamber window I called to Mr. John Fines my next neighbour, one of my Lord Say's brothers.[73] He was pleased to come to me, and two of his daughters, Mistress Susanna, and Mistress Hannah. I not being able to indure Mr. Hampson's railing went down stairs with Mistress Hannah into my parlour. Mr. Hampson thought I was gone out of the house, and came down. He met my maid in the entry, and said hussey where are the keys? He ran to the street door and locked it, but I was in the parlour. A little after Mr. Hampson went away not having an opportunity to turn me out of doors. By this time my moneys grew low, and I would not change my gold, but did send a suit of hangings to pawn by my cook-maid.[74] I put a chain upon my door, for I could hope for nothing but violence from Mr. Hampson. At last I was betrayed by my chamber-maid, and the foot-boy. My maid told me Mistress Hannah Fines lay a dying. I presently went to see her, for I knew she was sick. My maid at the same time desired me to let her go see an acquaintance, which I consented to. When I had been for some time at Mistress Fines chamber, the house-keeper came up to me, saying I was undone, for that Mr. Hampson was come with seven men unto my house and had shut up the doors and windows. I went and knocked at my door. All the answer Mr. Hampson made me was he said I had robbed him, but would not open the door. Them that were with him, I believe was his creditors, for I knew not of any enemy that I had. I heard that Sir Theodore de Veaux[75] was one, by my foot-boy, to whom they had promised great matters, but he was served as a traytor, turned off. The said Sir Theodore was a client to Mr. Hampson, and some say had an employment, rendered him enemy to honest women. The other as I suppose, was Mr. Henry Poulton, Mr. Edwards, Mr. Hopton Shuter, Mr. Powel, Mr. Hollman.[76] If they were not those men, I have reason to believe so, for Poulton and Hollman were the trustees in the joynture Mr. Hampson had taken from me, and when I spoke of it to them, they said they knew of no such trust. Mr. Hopton Shuter I have before given you an account of, how I was used by him at my own table, Mr. Powel and his wife assistants, and Mr. Hampson owed money to Mr. Edward. If it was these men or others, I hope God hath and will give them grace to repent, for assisting Mr. Hampson in such an unlawful, cruel, scandalous and ungrateful an action. Mr. Hampson took from me then an hundred and fifty pounds in gold, which my mother and grand-mother had kept as a jewel, it was old gold of several kings reigns, and jewels and cloaths to the value of much more. My house was in Southampton-Square, the next door to the Black-Moors-Head, near Kings Street in Bloomsbury. I went that night to lodge at one Mr. Heins's house of the Six Clarks-Office,[77] and the next day made my complaint in the spiritual court.[78] Mr. Hampson had caused so strongly to be reported that I was gone from him, that untill he came to the court, no person did credit what I said. When Mr. Hampson came into the court, Sir Giles Sweat,[79] which was then judge, told him he wondered at my complaint of him, for that he had known his father very well, and that they had been fellow collegians together, and desired him to speak for himself. Mr. Hampson did say that I was a high spirited woman, and had formerly called him cheat, and, once on a time at the Temple, had drawn a pen-knife through his hand and cut his finger, which he formerly complained of to Doctor Ball,[80] and scratched him in the face, and that now I denied him my mother's bonds and moneys. I answered all this to Mr. Hampson's shame. Sir Giles Sweat gave me five pounds a week, and gave him eight days' time to shew better cause for his turning me away, by some allegation. The time appointed, Mr. Hampson brought in none, but desired another week's time, which was granted, after which time he had composed an allegation of an old lye, how that I had gone into France some years before, without his consent. This allegation could not be lawfully admitted, had it been as true as I could then proved it to be false.[81] Yet by fraud and unjust favour, the said allegation was admitted, notwithstanding we had lived together some years since, the pretended offence, out of which was drawn the said allegation. And the judge's delegates,[82] to whom Mr. Hampson appealed, when he stood excommunicated in the Court of Arches,[83] did oblige me to answer

upon oath, contrary to the law of the land, the said allegation. Which I
did, and put in one against him, which I believe he never answered, for
I never heard any read against him in open court, nor saw him in the
court but once, which was after the death of honest Sir William Turner,
who dyed at Richmond just as the term began. He was faithful to me,
and had told Mr. Hampson in the open court that he was a knave, and
had endeavored by a bribe to gain him. In his death my case was lost.
Sir Walter Walker[84] was my other counsel who took fees, but would not
open his mouth to bring my case to a hearing, and did propose to me that
Mr. Hampson would allow me one hundred pound a year, if I would
consent that he should live from me a part, and that he did advise me to
agree to it. Which I did, not being able, for want of friends to bring my
case to a hearing, for Mr. Hampson so craftily ordered the matter, that
the Bishops and Common Lawyers came not together. For had my case
come then above board Mr. Hampson had been the scorn of all honest
men.[85] It was agreed upon between Mr. Hampson and myself, that I
should live where I pleased, and an act signed by him and me. So soon as
this was done, I desired Mr. John Fines, one of my Lord Saz's brothers
which lived next door to the house Mr. Hampson had turned me out of,
that he would return me my monys into France which favour he was
pleased to grant me. So soon as I was in France, Mr. Hampson said I was
dead,[86] or hid in London. Mr. Fines writ me these words to Paris, where
I then was. I sent speedily certificates from two publick notaries, and
signed by Mr. Vankesel, and Le Clere, and Mr. de Vouge, all three eminent banquers in Paris, and correspondents to Sir Laurance Debusty then
living in London.[87] These certificates Mr. Hampson told Mr. Fines were
counterfeited, and did pretend not to belive them, but continued to say I
was dead, to avoid the payment of my alimony. This troubled me very
much, for I had no desire to return for England, because Mr. Hampson
when he had with my consent, got the liberty to live apart from me, to
excuse himself to the world, said such things as the father of falsehood
suggested to him, and which he had not the presumption to speak of it in
court, being a thing unlike truth. For you may judge, had there been any-

thing but like a crime alledged, it would have been my ruin. I having no friend in court, nor any to speak or solicit for me, so, although innocent, I was cruelly turned off, and disgraced, and having no relations a live to support me. I thought it better for me to live where I was in good esteem, and to that end I spoke to the Dutches of Longville,[88] to give me her certificate, and the lady in whose house I lived Mademoiselle De Ports,[89] a maid of great quality, and cozen to the said Dutches. They were pleased to grant them me, and to send them to Mounsier Pompone, Secretary of State,[90] with order from the Dutches, that he should write to Monsier Colbert[91] which was then Embassador in England, to deliver them to whom I thought good. I desired they might be delivered to my Lord Chief Barron Montagu's lady,[92] because she had been pleased formerly to shew me great compassion, and much civility in my troubles. The said lady did me the favour to receive them from Monsier Colbert and send them to Mr. John Fines, who had my letter of attorny. The said Mr. Fines had so much charity for me as to carry them himself to Mr. Hampson, who when he saw them, fell into a great passion, and railed saying, "how could those persons know that I was his wife." And Mr. Fines being a man in years, Mr. Hampson took the advantage as he went down the stairs, and came behind him, did strike and abuse him. And when the old gentleman by the force of his courage strugled himself into a defensive posture, to make use of his cane, Mr. Hampson ran into his chamber and shut his door. Mr. Fines writ me word how Mr. Hampson had used him for his civility to me, and that he would not act any longer for me. Some time after a person of quality spoke to the King[93] to give me a letter of recommendation to his Majesty the King of England,[94] which was granted. Mr. Pompone offered me to take care that it should be presented to the King, which I refused, and sent it to Mr. Jolly by a friend in Paris. But finding I had no answer of it I was forced to go to England where I received my alimony, after some charge and trouble as he [Robert Hampson] hath untill these two years last past,[95] untill which time Sir Richard Lloyd[96] my counsel had a letter of attorny. But he told me Mr. Hampson was a rude man, and he did not care to solicit him, so that when I was

in France, about 1678[97] I was resolved to try how great a confidence I
should shew I had in Mr. Hampson, by addressing myself only to him,
would work on him; hoping that time and the consideration that he
ought to have, that it had been my estate that hath raised him in the
world and made him easie, it would without aid of any other advocate,
have perswaded him to pay that little alimony, his friends the Delegates[98]
had obliged me to consent too. But not hearing my complaint, I may term
them so. For my allegations against Mr. Hampson were never read in
court. Mr. Hampson had the advantage to know, the Bishops, Common
Lawyers, and Doctors, he choosed for his delegates,[99] by which means he
informed them what he pleased, and they never would hear me, for which
most of them gave an account not long after. For in a short time they
appeared before the great Tribunal,[100] and about two of twelve left, which
have been my judges these many years. The one was Mr. Hampson's
procter's brother,[101] the other I cannot complain of, not finding that he
had sacrificed to the Idol.[102] I may justly call Mr. Hampson so for he had
been an imposture to me, and abused the faith I had in him, and no just
man can take his part. For having thoroughly examined my case, they
must sacrifice their conscience, or condemn him. For I know not what
way to take to receive that poor livelihood I consented to. For the generous way which I was used whilst I was in France about 1678 turns to my
confusion, saying he received no letters from me at that time. And when I
came over, I had a great deal of trouble and charge before I could get him
cited, and when he was, he had so much business that he could not appear
nor shew the cause, untill the last day of Easter Term, about the year 1680.
Then I was appointed to be there at two of the clock after dinner, and
when I came my counsel told me, that Doctor Masters, Mr. Hampson's
counsel had alledged what he had to say in the morning. It was a libell
that one Mr. Edmund Everard had put in a book.[103] The said libell was
read in the court to make me odious. In the afternoon the two judges
delegates which are all that are living, as I have before related, did order
Mr. Hampson to pay thirty pounds of arrears, by the first day of the
term following. Then he pretended to bring in an allegation which was

only a pretence to put me to charge and troublesome delays, which my counsel could not help, because there was but two judges: Doctor Exton, and Doctor Pinfold. [104] The said Judge Exton was more inclined to mercy than justice, but the great mistake in the application made the action of no merit. His brother Mr. Hampson's proctor & may be they are misinformed, but the judge has two ears, and there is no excuse for such as incline to one side more than the other. I had no person to complain to, but my counsel whom I importuned, so much that Sir Richard Lloyd advised me to go to Mr. Hampson myself and demand my money. I did not willingly follow that advice, but being forced for want of bread to surmount the just aversion I had, to visit so unjust and so unreasonable a man, armed with the patience that the Almighty did in mercy give me, I went to his chambers at the Temple, where I found only a young boy, who having not then been otherwise instructed, or it may be knew me not, prayed me come in, and wait untill his Master came, (which would not be long). After half an hour there came a boy to inquire if there were any body to speak with Mr. Serjant Hampson, the boy said yes, a gentlewoman. After three hours waiting his cleark appeared to me, his hat fast on his head,[105] and with insolence asked me what I did there. Within a while afterwards came in Mr. Hampson, with the furious looks of a man that would seem to out-brave an apperation.[106] I hoped to have calmed his raging spirit by a moderate discourse, and said to him I was sorry that he did force me to give him the trouble, to come in person to demand that small alimony I had consented to receive, and which was by agreement to be paid every quarter in the Temple-Hall, and that I hoped he was fully satisfied since I had by an act in court given him the liberty to live apart from me. And that he was in free possession of my mother's estate, and of that my uncle left me, he would out of respect to my deceased mother & uncle, (who as he said) had so great love for him, as to give him an estate which made him live easie in the world, that he would be pleased to consider that I belonged to those persons that had made him happy. He made me no answer, but sent his cleark to call to him Mr. Richard Edwards and one Robinson[107] which were at hand. So soon as they were in the chamber, Mr. Hampson shut the door, and said that I came to molest him, and did strike me upon the head to the ground; then threw me against a glass-door. Feeling myself hurt in the arm with the glass (although much ashamed) I cryed out. The two men Edwards and Robinson stood as applauders of Mr. Hampson. When I cryed out Mr. Hampson opened his inward chamber door, and there was his cleark and another man, ready at Mr. Hampson's order to drag me into the street. And at the Temple Gate, the cleark said I was mad, and that they had order to bring me to Bedlam. The multitude came about me and began to pull and tear what I had on. I had an earring tore out of my ear, and had not a woman that came by, put me into a coffee-house at the Temple Gate, I had been murthered by the rabble. After I had recovered my strength and was returning to my lodging, Mr. Hampson's cleark followed me to St. Clements Church, but durst come no further, because I lodged thereabouts. After this shameful usage I thought it not safe for me (that had no more near relations alive nor friend to protect me against Mr. Hampson's rage and violent proceedings) to let him know where I dwell. So that every time I received alimony it is with so great charges and trouble, that with pain can I subsist upon it. The last time I did receive my alimony, it was by virtue of an excommunication which the court could not refuse me. But when it was to be signed, Doctor Exton was not in the way, Doctor Pinfold signed it without difficulty and with great importunity, Mr. Franklin's cleark brought me to a tavern where Doctor Exton was. I presented him my excommunication which he refused to sign, and moreover told me it should not be done whilst I was in London, so justice was stopped. But Mr. Hampson knowing it would not so stand sent my moneys to Mr. Franklin's chamber. Since which time I have been out of England, and sent Mr. Hampson several letters, and the procuration made by a publick notary to Mr. Francis Burk, Merchant in London. His answer to Mr. Burk was, he would not pay unless he know the place and house where I lived,[108] and that I should call in this Relations which I caused to be printed at Rotterdam about the year 1680.[109] A very unnecessary demand, because he had sent the said Everard to Rotterdam who did lodge at Mr. Godens's[110] house the printer where my books were printed, and when I sent to a merchant to pay the remainder of the moneys due, and send me my books, the merchant sent word that Mr. Everard had caused all to be burned.[111] It must be by Mr. Hampson's means, for the said Everard had no power, nor was in a condition to subborn the printer. After this Mr. Hampson sent me word, I should have no moneys unless I called in my books.

All these and many other false and cruel actions which Mr. Hampson hath practised to oppress my innocence, and make me miserable in this world, does and hath assured me, and will in Gods good time, make appear unto all good and intelligent persons, that Mr. Hampson's leaving of me was a cruel, scandalous, and malicious desertion, which by the laws of all countrys sets the innocent party free.[112]

I was turned away in a cruel and inhumane manner, against the law of God and the land, and that Mr. Hampson is very sensible of, for which cause he does not only make it his business to keep me in a poor condition, so that I cannot appear like myself,[113] but does his endeavour to make me pass for a mad-woman, and smother the truth of my case and myself together, that his actions may not come to light. But my confidence is in the eternal Judge, before whom the impure shall not stand. There is my comfort in my great affliction, which I have suffered from my infancy.[114] For I was no other when he betrayed me to himself, and out of all my worldly goods into a strange country, where I lived without spot, and truly innocent of that sin which is the dishonour of my sex, for which my soul doth bless the Lord, and all that is within me praise his holy Name, who hath preserved my life from destruction, and crowned me with loving kindness, and tender mercies.

The cleark which had the impudence to lay violent hands on me, took books up in Mr. Hampson's name, at Mr. Lees at the Temple-Gate, and left him his name was Chelbery of Taplow[115] parents as I am informed.

Now Courteous Reader, I shall give you an account, of when, and how, I came to know such a man as Mr. Edmund Everard, whom I should not trouble myself once to mention, was he not one of the chief instruments Mr. Hampson employs against me.

About the year 1671 having consented by force that Mr. Hampson should live by himself & I liberty to live where I pleased, I returned to France, where I hoped to have lived in a peaceable retirement, but the Almighty thought it not good for me. There passed at that time in the packet-boat two old Irish men, and they amongst other travellers went in the same stage-coach to Paris. I being the only person that spoke English, they did discourse with me. When the coach arrived at Paris I would not appear to my acquaintance, being discomposed with my journey, but went to a lodging where the coach arrived. The two old men, having never as they said been at Paris, nor speaking one word of French came into the same house, untill they sent and inquired after their friends and acquaintance. The next evening after I came to Paris, the mistress of the house desired I would come and sup in the hall, assuring me there was only my two country men, (as she named them) and a young man of their acquaintance. I did go down and after supper, one of the men told me the young man's name was Everard a kinsman of his. The said Mr. Everard addressed himself to me, telling me he had a great desire to render all the service his poor condition would admit of to all English, and that he never was in England, but if he could get to serve some English man of quality,[116] he should think himself very happy. He said he served Monsier de la Renee, Lieutenant de la Pottice, and that Madam de la Renee was one of the modestest women in Paris, and that if I wanted a taylor, or a shooe-maker, he would bring hers to me, which I did not refuse. And finding him very oficious,[117] I having then no servant did send him of several messages. For Mr. Hampson having taken my cloths, I wanted many things necessary before I could appear. So soon as I was cloathed I wanted moneys. And one day being in a lady's house of my acquaintance, I gave the said Everard a gold watch to carry to pawn. He brought me some moneys, upon which I gave him in a short time to redeem it. He told me the person to whom he had pawned it, said the time was out, and would not return the watch. I asked him for the moneys which I gave him to redeem it which I could not have. He gave me an acknowledgement under his hand, which I valued not from such a person. After this action

I saw him not for some time. After which the said Everard brought to me the news that Mr. Hampson's nephew, Mr. Thomas Laurence[118] was in Paris. I was glad of the news, for he having seen me, Mr. Hampson could not with any colour say I was dead. Mr. Laurence did tell me that Mr. Hampson would pay the moneys, if I would send an acquittance[119] to England, before I received the moneys. I acquainted an advocate in Paris of the proposal. The said advocate did advise me not to do it. His lady, before she married him was a widdow of quality which had known me of a long time, & was so moved to compassion seeing how I was oppressed did by her credit at the French Court, obtain me a letter of recommendation, from the King unto the King of England, and being at St. Germains to solicit for my letter, as I was going to Monsier Pompone's lodgings, which was then Secretary of State, I met the said Everard. He was cloathed like a gentleman, and desired I would suffer that he might give me his hand up to Mr. Pompone's lodgings, who so soon as he saw me, said Madam, tomorrow at the Kings rising your letter shall be signed. Till this time I do verily believe that the said Everard had not so much as heard that I was to have a letter from the King although he hath published in his book that he had obtained me that grace in the French Court. When I was returned I asked the said Everard how he came into so good a condition, and what he did there. He told me he had or did serve the Duke of Monmouth.[120] I asked how he came so prefered. He said by my Lady Hamelton,[121] and shewed me three letters which he said was hers to him, and a card of the nine of hearts with a mysterious writing upon it. I was in wonder as his discourse. For although I had not the honour to know my Lady Hamelton, I believed nothing ill of the lady, but believed him to be what he was, and hath proved himself to the world. He likewise plucked a book out of his pocket, which he said had been written by Pope Lyon, and that in it there were charms of all sorts, and that there was but that and one more in France, which the Duke of Anguien the Princes son had, which was the cause the Duke never received an wound in the war, and that the said book had been condemned to be burnt. I had a great mind to read in the book, but it was Latin. He told me he had it from an

Italian that lived in Paris which had a great esteem of him, & had given him many secrets.[122] I let him run on in his discourse, believing he prated only to divert me from speaking to him of my watch. He said he could make such powder, that a pistol or gun should be shot off without noise.[123] He said likewise he could kill any person at a distance by making their image in clay, & by pricking the image upon the place of the heart. By little and little the person should die in a languishing condition. I thought the said Everard told me these things as a romance,[124] but now I find his design was not good. The next morning I had my letter and went to Paris. But receiving no good by it, I did declare to my acquaintance that I would speedily go for England. And a very little time before I went over, the said Everard came to me in a very humble manner, and prayed me that I would assist him in his journey to England, for that he was resolved to go, and that he would submit to wear a livery,[125] if I would let him wait on me to England. I told him my fortune was too small. He said he wanted bread, and in truth I was moved to compassion, and did give him a dinner such as I had. He continued his request to me that I would be pleased to let him serve me as a foot-man. I wondered at his request, he being not contented to serve Monsier de la Renyes nephew, and lived in a house where there was no want of what was convenient for servants. So I durst not take him but took a little French boy. The said Everard then told me he would go for England if he begged by the way. He seemed to me to be in a desperate condition which I knew not the cause of, never knowing any of his affairs. A day or two after I arrived at London, having occasion to be out of the house, when I came in, Mr. Fines his house-keeper, told me there had been to speak with me a young man newly come from France, and had letters for me from the Dutches of Longville, and from the Countiss of Montperuse. The next day about eleven of the clock, the said Everard was brought unto my chamber, so soon as I saw him I asked him for my letters. He said he had not any, and that he said so to have admittance to speak with me. I saw him in so trembling and mortified a condition,[126] that I asked him if he were sick. He said no only indisposed, by reason of a slight wound he received in a dispute with one

Mr. Mecarty[127]; I asked him what he did in England, and where he lived.
He answered he was lodged in the Temple. Then I began to be afraid of
him, and called to mind his discourse at St. Germans, how he had said he
could shoot off a pistol without noise, and did not believe he was
wounded in his hand, but that he had some ill design because of his trembling. He desired that my foot-boy who was in the chamber, might help
him with a glass of small-beer. I looked upon the boy who was intelligent
and saw that I was afraid and did not go out of the chamber. Two or three
days after, there came one of the messengers of the chamber from White-
Hall, to let me know I must come to Mr. Secretary's lodgings. I was com-
forted with this summons, hoping his Majesty had received the Kings
letter in my behalf, and was pleased to take my deplorable condition into
his consideration. When I came to Mr. Secretary Coventry's[128] chambers,
I found nothing of what with reason and justice I expected. There was
only my Lord of Bath,[129] and the Secretary, who asked me if I knew one
Everard. I answered yes. He told me that the said Everard was taken with
several sorts of poison about him, and that he said I had subborned him
to poison Mr. Hampson, and for his recompence I had promised him my
daughter in marriage, and a hundred pounds that lay in Sir Laurence de
Busty's hands.[130] I told my Lord of Bath, and Mr. Secretary, that as to the
hundred pounds, Sir Laurence de Busty could satisfy them as to the falseness of that invention, and that I did not question, but the circumstance
of my case would justifie me to all unbiased and reasonable persons. For
I had a joynture made before marriage, and notwithstanding I have consented to the sale of it. I am debared of my thirds,[131] so that after his
death I have nothing to live upon, and whilst he lives the law will give me
a livelihood, to what end should I wish for his death.[132] I am a woman
that at the age of twenty years was grown old with grief and sorrow, for I
was not weaned from all worldly consolations as now I am, who have
consumed many years in the privation of all earthly comforts. I desire all
un-prejudged persons, to judge what I could propose to myself of good
in Mr. Hampson's death. I told my Lord of Bath, that I had designed to
retire very speedily out of London, and asked him if I might do it, with-

out giving suspicion against my innocence. He was pleased to tell me I might freely retire, and in truth, I thought no more of Everard. But about four years after, lodging at one Mr. Philips a Grocer at the three Sugar-Loaves over against Summerset-House, upon a Sunday morning before I was out of my bed there knocked a person at my door very boldly. I asked who was there, a voice answered your servant Everard. I desired him to retire. It was winter, & in the evening as it began to be dark, he came up the stairs and into my chamber without knocking. I bless God I was not alone, but discoursing with a poor woman that lodged in the house, and staid that day by me, because that afternoon, I had new cause of afflic-tion. Mr. Charles le Gard[133] that lodged in Summerset-House had been with me, to let me know that the Saturday before the evening, at the time he was with the Queen at Service in the chappel, his chambers were bro-ken up, and nothing stole but my box and a little trunck of writings, which belonged to his brother in law Mr. Cranmer, which trunck had H.W. upon it. He desired that I should tell him what was in my box, for that he would put it in the News-Book,[134] which was done. And I be-lieved le Gard honest, untill a day after when I went to the said le Gards chambers, accompanied with one Sir Richard Elsworth,[135] and a Porter to bring away a glass of mine that was also in his chambers. It was in the morning. He came himself to the door, but I was heartily surprised, when I saw a night-gown upon his back of the same striped Indian sattin, which I had several pieces of in the box I had intrusted him with, where were also all my writings and proofs against Mr. Hampson. Then I had no reason but to believe I was betrayed. I had then a petecoat of the same satin which I showed to Sir Richard Elsworth and the porter. I asked Mr. le Gard where he bought of his night-gown, he said, at the Old-Exchange. I should have brought the said le Gard before my Lord of Ossery the Queen's Chamberlin,[136] but he was that day upon his depart to Holland. I did not name le Gard in the first impression,[137] although his action is set down in the beginning of this Relation.

The said Everard after he had so stole into my chamber, spoke in French. I told him I would not discourse with him, but if he had anything to say to me, he must speak in English. For I would not hear anything from him, but what the woman should be witness of. Some time after I heard he had writ a book and made use of my name in it,[138] and since I find he is an instrument for Mr. Hampson, and hath as I am informed caused this Relation to be burnt at Rotterdam.

These proceedings of Mr. Hampson after the agreement made betwixt us, obliges me to believe that he seeks my life, and the more strongly because he pretends not to believe any person that I am living nor certificates. I hope God will give him a sight of his malicious persecution of me, or raise me up some good samaritan that will assist me in my destitute condition. But whatever his Almighty providence hath ordained; I comfort myself with his Promise that he will lay no more affliction upon me than I shall be able to support.

A little before the said le Gard pretended that his chambers were broke up, and my box stole, I had intrusted him with my keys, and desired him to bring me a bundle of papers which were in the box. When I had looked them over, and saw there was the receipt of my portion, and my mother's bonds and letters enough to prove how falsely Mr. Hampson had dealt with me, I desired the said le Gard to put them again into the box untill such time as I had need and them, and did unwisely declare to him, that my design was to put a bill in Chancery in a kinsman's name against Mr. Hampson, and set forth the fact.[139]

Thus hath my simplicity been betrayed, because I have wanted the wisdom of the Serpent. But certainly it is not by chance that such a man as Mr. Hampson was ordained to be so great a cross to me. For in him I lost all the pretensions, my youth, education, birth, and fortune could have pretended to. And I confess my passion predominent was ambition, and the love of glory, which made my disgrace and want so much the more sensible and insupportable to me. And I do look upon it as a very great mercy from the Almighty that he hath given me strength to bear so many crosses, and to undergo so great and many afflictions without falling into a destracted condition, and hath learned me in my tryal, to know that the glory of this world is only vanity and vexation of spirit, and hath let me see the folly of those that commit crimes to profess them, and have reason to hope that I may say, *It is good for me that I have been afflicted.*[140] And if it is not the Almighty's will to restore me any worldly comforts, he will as the last justifie me, to those that are as Jobs Comforters to me, judge me guilty because of my sufferings. But my hope and comfort is that the Lord God shall judge me who knows my integrity, and in whose mercy I trust.

Die Lunæ viz Vicessimo Secundo die Mensis Maii Anno Domini, 1671.[141] Coram Dominis Exton, Clark & Pinfold, Delegatis, &c. in aula publica infra ædes Exoniences in le Strand in commitatu Middlesex inter horas deciman & duodecimam ante meridiem præsente Thoma Oughton Notario Publico, &c.

Hampson con Hampson
Exton [and] Franklin[142]

Which day appeared personally before the Judges Delegates above specified.

Robert Hampson Esquire and Mary Hampson his wife, and the said Mr. Hampson did pay to his said wife, the sum of forty and eight pounds, in full satisfaction of all sums due for alimony, after the rate of fifty shillings a week, set by the court. And he the said Robert Hampson did promise, contract and agree, to pay unto the said Mary Hampson his wife or her assigns upon demand in the Inner-Temple-Hall, one hundred pounds of lawful mony of England a year, during their joynt lives, by quarterly payments; the first quarter to begin on the eighth day of June next, so as he may have full liberty and freedom to live by himself and apart from her, and that he not be sued or molested by any person or persons for any monys, goods, wares or commodities taken up or received by her for the time to come. And he also agreed and consented, that in case he failed to pay and perform as aforesaid, he shall then be and stand excommunicated if being called by the Court (which is to be at his charge) he doth not shew good cause to the contrary. He did also agree and consent that she shall have full liberty and freedom to live by herself

apart from him where she pleaseth, without any suit, trouble or molesta-
tion by him to be made or had any time for the future. To all which the
said Mrs. Hampson did give her full and free consent, and did promise
and bind herself to perform and fulfill all that is on her part to be performed; and did accept the said one hundred pounds a year during their
joynt lives; and did give her consent that he shall have liberty to live by
himself apart from her, without any suit or trouble to be made or given
him by her in that behalf; and that he shall not be troubled or molested
by any person, for any mony by her to be borrowed, or by any debt by her
to be incurred any time hereafter, which if he be, that then he shall and
may stop so much of such mony or quarterly payments as shall become
due unto her for the annuity above mentioned. As touching the process,
the judges do ratifie confirm and allow of and decree, that the same shall
take effect and be performed by both parties, especially during their joynt
lives, without any contradiction, controul or process to be had or made at
any time hereafter to the contrary, touching their living apart as aforesaid,
and touching the alimony to be paid by him to her, quarterly as aforesaid.

*Being ill advised I consented to this agreement. For as it doth appear there is no
penalty against Mr. Hampson but excommunication; where he suffers and stands excommunicated, and I have not bread to live on,*[143]

Robert Hampson, Mary Hampson.
Vera Copia Examinata per me Thomas Oughton Not. Pub. Reg.
Regium.[144]

The CASE

OF

Mrs. Mary Hampson

EXAMINED

PERSPECTIVES $\&$ AFTERMATH

Chapter 1

THE HAMPSON MARRIAGE

Competing Stories

Mary Hampson's pamphlet, or book as she always called it, tells the story of her troubled marriage with Robert Hampson from her perspective. But this was not the only place where the story of this marriage was told. In two courts—the Court of Arches, and the High Court of Delegates—Mary and Robert Hampson give their own, often conflicting, versions of events. Here the circumstances of their early meeting and early married life are presented. Here also are conflicting versions of the violence that marred this marriage, and behavior that society would consider undesirable. In these court cases they present differing stories of Robert's first beating of Mary, his neglect of her, and her journey to France. In discussing later conflicts, Mary, in her testimony, insists that after their second reconciliation in 1668 she submitted to Robert's authority and resumed all the duties of a wife. Robert in his responses accuses Mary of continued shrewishness and dishonesty. In court testimony, Mary also accuses Robert of stealing the inheritance her mother intended to leave her, and of attempting to destroy her relationship with her mother. Finally the last days of the marriage are described in court documents. Here we see the end of the Hampson marriage, with Mary locked out of her house and accused before a justice of the peace with the very real possibility of imprisonment. These are the stories that are told in court testimony, which sometimes support and sometimes challenge the version of events that Mary Hampson tells in her published narrative of her marriage.

In her letter to Sir William Trumbull dated 20 October 1680,[1] Mary Hampson declared that she believed she would be forced to tell her story to the world in print. It would have been more accurate to say she intended to present her version of events to the world. In her pamphlet, Mary Hampson took possession of the story of her marriage in an attempt to give her marital trials a central purpose. In order to do this, she presents her suffering as part of a predestined path through which she triumphs as a heroine of adversity—where her struggles become a sign of God's spiritual design for her, rather than the result of her human vulnerability. More practically, the pamphlet provided an opportunity for Mary to defend herself and express the anger and frustration she felt toward Robert and her society more generally. The court testimony presents a much more detailed and complex version of events.

The first public airing of the story of this disastrous marriage was in the ecclesiastical Court of Arches, with a second hearing coming a few months later in a court of appeals—the High Court of Delegates—where Robert sought to reverse the Court of Arches decision that ordered him to fulfill his responsibilities as a husband to support Mary financially and live with her peaceably. Other records and documents, including parish records, lawsuits, and a small inscription on the slab covering the grave of Mary's youngest daughter Anne, also contribute to a more complete and complex picture of the Hampsons' life together than Mary chose to present in her pamphlet. However, these documents contain their own limitations as well, produced as they were in particular circumstances for particular purposes.

Depositions taken by the various courts of the period were written according to a fixed structure, which could reveal as well as hide certain aspects of the situation being described. The language and the imagery found in Mary's deposition at times seem unnatural. In the legal setting, people like Mary would draw on language found in religious teachings, conduct manuals, and legal practice in the hope that their testimony would carry more weight and bring about a positive outcome for them. Word choice, the level and type of detail, the order in which the events were told, and the emphasis given to particular aspects of their stories all contributed to how the testimony of each individual was perceived and had a direct bearing on the result of the legal action. This understanding of the importance of how one told one's story to the courts appears to have been widespread in the culture. The tense nature of legal actions, which pitted an individual against another, demanded that people craft their responses carefully. Despite this, court testimony did establish a core of agreed fact. The story that Mary tells in her depositions should be accepted as generally the truth as she saw it.

How one carried oneself while giving a deposition could also influence legal decisions. Both Mary and Robert were aware that their behavior as they met with the court officials and staff, and the manner in which they responded to questions, could affect the judgment to come. For Mary, the experience of telling her story in this setting must have been particularly daunting. She would have been brought to a room or chamber, surrounded by men, where a court official would have asked her the set questions of the deposition. A legal clerk would have taken down her answers and recast them into a third-person narrative. He would also add legal terms and repetitions, and he would have phrased her responses according to legal convention. Mary would then have been shown the written text containing her answers. At times there is evidence she added information, which the scribe then wrote into the margins. This situation generally would have been stressful enough for Mary. However, there was also the fact that Robert was a gifted lawyer in his own right and a man well practiced in legal rhetoric and strategy. He also, coincidentally, had taken rooms in Exeter House, where (after the Great Fire of 1666) much of the legal business of the Court of Arches was being carried out in rented chambers. Mary would have been keenly aware that she was stepping into Robert's space—both because he resided there and because it was the world of the law. She knew that her answers and the way she carried herself within this environment would have consequences so fundamental that her very existence as a gentlewoman literally hung in the judicial balance. In this tense and contentious environment emerged a record of the discord, the disagreements, and the raw and painful moments of the Hampson marriage that Mary sought to reshape more fully (to her own advantage) when she wrote the story of her marriage for publication in 1684.

In Mary's printed story, *A Plain and Compendious Relation of the Case of Mrs. Mary Hampson*, the marriage sounds doomed from the beginning. Here she condenses her courtship and early marriage into a few sentences, with adversity arriving quickly at her door. Yet court testimony reveals this was not actually the case. It confirms that in the autumn or early winter of 1655–56 Robert Hampson came to the house of the widow Elizabeth Wingfield with the intention of obtaining permission to wed the young Mary. Robert was twenty-nine years old and a rising lawyer who had just inherited a substantial interest in land that he believed would make him a fortune. Robert's father, Sir Thomas Hampson, had heavily invested in the Bedford Levels Project to drain the marshy fenlands of East Anglia. Mary recounts in her pamphlet that Robert "came to Chatres [Chatteris] in the Isle of Ilee [Ely], to look after his fenlands, and lay at a ministers house, an acquaintance of my mothers, which minister brought him to see me with the reputation of a man of very considerable estate, his father's only executor." She prefaces this comment with the lament "by sad misfortune to me." Elizabeth Wingfield, along with her brother Thomas Whalley and her sister-in-law Sarah Whalley, was delighted with the prospect of a marriage between Mary and this prosperous lawyer from a good family. It is very likely at the time that Mary was just as pleased with the proposed marriage.

In the society of seventeenth-century England, marriage was an important familial institution. It bound not only the marital couple but also their extended families into a relationship of mutual aid and support. Through marriage, families enhanced their standing in their communities, their financial prospects, their political security, and even their personal well-being. And even though the many books on matrimony and marital relations stressed the importance of a supportive and companionate marriage between two people, everyone accepted that marriage had consequences far beyond the immediate marital household. Robert Hampson's appearance in the parlor of Elizabeth Wingfield's modest gentry house suggested possibilities for social advancement and security that Elizabeth and Mary could not have expected to find while living quietly in their provincial town.

Mary herself recalled that in her youth she had expectations in line with her birth and fortune. These certainly would have included a marriage that would advance her socially and place her in the highest social circles. Mary was the only child and heir of Bodenham Wingfield, son of Sir James Wingfield of Kimbolton Castle. Mary's ancestor, Charles Wingfield, favored by Henry VIII, had played host to the discarded Katherine of Aragon, who spent the last eighteen months of her life at Kimbolton. Thus Mary had pretentions that came from her membership in a long-established gentry family. Unfortunately, Bodenham also came from a large family and was the second son. He took a degree from Cambridge but appears to have been content to live the life of a provincial gentleman, surviving on the modest income his father had provided, rather than seeking his fortune at law or as a scholar. Bodenham also died young, while still in his twenties, less than a month after Mary's birth. Mary's mother, Elizabeth, never remarried, choosing instead to raise Mary in the small town of Chatteris rather than seek the social advancement that could have come from marrying again.

Yet, despite Elizabeth Wingfield's reluctance to remarry, she would certainly have accepted her responsibility to arrange a suitable marriage for Mary. Robert Hampson was the second son of a baronet, with a promising legal career. In addition, he had a fresh inheritance in what appeared to be the fortune-making project of the century. All of this made him appear to be an ideal marital prospect for the young Mary. As for Robert, Mary's modest inheritance made her suitable, but her real attraction would have been her family connections. The Hampson family had only recently entered into the ranks of the upper gentry. Marriage with Mary would align Robert with a more established gentry family and place him in an excellent position for social advancement.

In her pamphlet, Mary states that several women refused to marry Robert before he came to Chatteris, and there may have been some truth to Mary's accusation. It is possible Robert may not have been a particularly attractive spouse to the class of gentlewomen he pursued before he received his inheritance. It is likely that Elizabeth Wingfield and John Whalley would not have seriously considered Robert for Mary were he only a lawyer with just his wages to live on. The death of Sir Thomas Hampson in 1655 changed all of this, when he left Robert substantial property and the Hampsons' London house. Mary also accuses Robert of presenting himself as possessing more wealth than he actually had, and though he certainly misrepresented his financial health because of his overconfidence in the fenland project, he was the executor of his father's estate and did inherit the bulk of Sir Thomas Hampson's non-entailed property.[2] In his will, Sir Thomas made it clear that he believed his eldest son, Thomas, to be unworthy and his second son, Robert, more ambitious and hard-working.[3] Thus Robert's apparently large inheritance from his father boded well for the future of the couple. And although Mary's printed version of her story leaves very little room to imagine a period of marital harmony, other documents suggest that the early years of the Hampson marriage were a period of hope and contentment.

The couple married in August 1656 and moved directly into the Hampsons' London house in Holborn road that Robert had recently inherited. Just nine months later, in April 1657, their first daughter, Elizabeth, was born. Her baptism is recorded in the parish register of St. Andrew's church, Holborn, which also notes that their home was near the Cross Keys Inn in Holborn.[4] Their second child, a son Robert, was born fifteen months later in 1658 and was also baptized at St. Andrews. During this time, Mary notes that two of Robert's sisters lived with them. It is likely that one of these sisters was Katherine Hampson, who remained unmarried and later became the foster mother of Mary's daughter Elizabeth.

For a little over two years, the family lived a comfortable gentry life in the Holborn townhouse, with Mary unaware of the financial firestorm waiting to erupt. During this time Mary was mistress of her own home, enjoyed the company of Robert's sisters and another family that lodged with them, and had the visible status of a well-born gentlewoman who had just given birth to her first son. This was the life Elizabeth Wingfield and Thomas Whalley hoped to secure for Mary when they arranged her marriage to Robert Hampson. When a fight between Robert and his sisters broke out in his study one night, Mary could not know that it signaled the end of her settled and contented life. It was only in retrospect, when Mary wrote her account of this evening nearly twenty years later, that she recognized the events of that night were an end to her youthful expectations and the beginning of the suffering she was to endure.

In her pamphlet, Mary explains that this argument between Robert and his sisters concerned money he was supposed to pay them for their share of the fenland property left by their father. The pamphlet does not go into further details concerning these fenlands, but court documents in the lawsuits Robert's siblings filed against him fill in many details.[5] From these documents we learn that Sir Thomas's fenlands included 219 acres in Raveley Fen (lot 11) and 296 acres of Rough Westmoor (lot 19). According to Sir Thomas Hampson's will, Robert was allowed to purchase his siblings' share of this property for two thousand pounds. At the time this was a reasonable financial agreement, given the wild optimism of the profits to be made from draining the fenlands. Unfortunately, this optimism was misplaced. The draining of the fenlands was never particularly successful, and the land that emerged from the swampy fens was useful only as poor grazing land, not the rich and valuable agricultural land the project had envisioned. Robert was never to recoup his investment in the fenlands. In 1694 Robert's daughters, Elizabeth and Mary, sold the Raveley Fen acreage for a hundred pounds,[6] less than a tenth of the price Robert had paid to his sisters for it. Sir Thomas Hampson's act of generosity in settling the fenlands on Robert with the stipulation that he buy his siblings out ended up having disastrous financial and personal consequences for Robert and Mary, and later for their two daughters.

Mary claims in her pamphlet that the Rough Westmoor acreage that made up part of her first jointure was encumbered by debt. Sadly, this was true. The legal actions of Robert's siblings prove that before his marriage he had not paid them the two thousand pounds for their portions of the fenlands. In other words, Robert was guilty of misleading Mary and her family before the marriage. He included property in the marriage agreement that was not paid for yet and thus was useless as a guarantee of future income for Mary should he die. This eventually led Mary to accuse her uncle, John Whalley, of being naïve and careless with respect to her financial well-being. Mary suggests that Whalley should have investigated Robert's financial situation more thoroughly before agreeing to the marriage settlement. But those accusations are not well founded. Whalley held back property he had agreed to settle on the couple once they were married, as a guarantee that Robert would fulfill his financial obligations toward Mary, which suggests he may have been aware that Robert had not yet settled all the financial issues related to the fenland property. It was not unusual for a family that invested money in a couple to exercise some control over the financial dealings of the husband by withholding property or money until they were satisfied all the obligations agreed to in the marriage settlement were met.

In 1659, John Whalley was no doubt relieved he had withheld the property promised to the couple. After the fight with his sisters, Robert Hampson insisted that Mary sign away her rights to the fenland property, which was part of her jointure. She claims in her pamphlet that she did this willingly, hoping to help her husband out of a difficult financial situation. John Whalley, when he heard that Mary had no jointure (a necessary financial agreement to protect her and her children should Robert die), demanded that Robert provide Mary a new jointure. Whalley threatened to keep property he had promised to give to Robert and Mary if Robert refused. Robert did provide a new jointure, the second jointure as she always called it. Whalley then agreed to give to them some of the property he had promised the couple, but not all of it.[7] And rather than giving the property to Robert immediately by deed, instead he willed it to Mary upon his death, which occurred in 1664.[8] Robert was able to claim the income of this property during his lifetime because he was Mary's husband.

However, he could never sell the property and the rent from it provided Mary with her only income after Robert's death.[9] The fact that Whalley did not deed the property directly to Robert suggests he had begun to distrust Robert and wished to secure at least a small income for Mary should Robert die without providing for her financially. As it turns out, Whalley's decision saved Mary from complete destitution in her old age.

In Mary's pamphlet she presents the early damage to the marriage as resulting from Robert's fraudulent and incompetent money dealings. He was certainly both financially optimistic and not completely forthcoming about his finances, however he was also incredibly unlucky. The fenland property did not return the easy profit he was led to believe it would by both his father and other respected investors—including the Earl of Bedford. Robert had believed this profit would allow him to quickly clear his debts to his brothers and sisters as well as other debts he had incurred. In 1659 Robert's sister Katherine was unwilling to wait any longer for her money; she brought a suit against her brother.[10] Her siblings, Ambrose, George, and Margaret, joined her in another suit the next year. The money Robert owed his brothers and sisters was now compounded by legal costs related to these suits. On top of these financial problems, Robert and Mary's infant son died (sometime between 1658 and 1660).

Within a very short period, Robert Hampson experienced the collapse of his financial expectations and the death of his young son and heir. His response was to break up his household and place Mary and the young Elizabeth in lodgings, and travel for months at a time on the legal circuit and on other business.[11] He probably went away frequently even in the early years of their marriage, but in these years Mary would have had the company of his sisters, and she was the mistress of a substantial London house. After Robert moved her into lodgings, Mary would have felt isolated from her social circle and have experienced financial insecurity for the first time in her life. She was also pregnant again and caring for her young daughter Elizabeth in these new circumstances.

To add to Mary's distress, Robert's financial dealings continued to cause problems. In July 1661 officers of Parliament came to her lodgings and demanded that she turn over the Roll of Statutes books for 1634–1640,[12] which had been kept by Robert's father and bequeathed to Robert. Again, Robert had paid his siblings for exclusive rights to the books only to find that they were of no financial worth and were in fact government property. The officers who appeared at Mary's door threatened to fine and imprison Robert if he refused to return the Statutes books. Mary's description of this incident in her pamphlet is supported by the records of the House of Lords, which list two officers going to the Hampsons' lodging at the time Mary describes.[13] It is not difficult to imagine that this visitation of officers frightened the heavily pregnant Mary and made her even less certain of her husband's trustworthiness and financial solvency. The episode also led to the first recorded incident of marital violence.[14]

One morning in June or July 1663, her pamphlet tells us, Mary attempted to discuss their financial affairs with Robert. She describes how he grew angry and "said I reproached him, and did strike me upon the breast which grew very bad." Court documents reveal a more harrowing and contested version of events. In the initial Court of Arches deposition, Mary claimed that Robert struck her on the breast when she was pregnant and that the beating put her life in danger. Robert replied that he had not hit Mary. Instead he claimed her breasts had become sore because of her pregnancy and that she had recovered from this condition before the birth of their daughter Anne. In the High Court of Delegates deposition, Mary provided greater detail still, claiming that when they lodged near Somerset House in London, "Robert did in a violent manner and with great cruelty give her, being with child and within three months of her delivery, a great blow upon her right breast which caused the same to swell greatly and the same thereby became very sore," bringing her close to death. Mary also claims here that Robert provided no financial or medical support for her, abandoning her in a weak and pregnant condition: "He unmercifully left her sick of that blow and came not to her for a good space of time and that being so left by her said husband without his taking care or providing for her she was fain to have recourse to her mother and friends for support and maintenance."[15] Again, in his answer to this claim, Robert responded that Mary had a sore breast, that he had not hit her, and that she had recovered by the time she delivered the infant Anne. He makes no comment on her claims that he left her without provision.

In this testimony, we see Mary and Robert constructing their stories for particular purposes.[16] Both the first court case in the Court of Arches and the second in the appellate High Court of Delegates (where Robert appealed the decision in the Court of Arches that found he was financially responsible for Mary) attempted to establish what rights Mary could claim from her husband, most especially the right to financial maintenance. The courts could order the couple to return to cohabitation, or allow the two to live separately, with or without financial support for the wife. The best a woman could expect in bringing her accusations of abuse to the ecclesiastical courts was the right to live separately and receive money to live on. In order to secure this judgment, a woman had to prove excessive cruelty or abandonment. A man was relieved of his marital duty to live with his wife and support her financially if he could prove her adultery, abandonment, or uncontrollable violence. The escalation of Mary's story of Robert's violence in her High Court of Delegates deposition reflects the importance for women of proving cruelty. In this deposition, Mary tells the delegates that when Robert beat her she was pregnant, and that she was left without proper medical care or provision. She describes how she was forced to seek the support of friends, family, and even strangers. This version of events placed Robert in clear breach of both customary and legal expectations regarding the treatment of a wife, and it better established Mary's right to maintenance. Mary is also careful to name individuals in order to establish the truth of her testimony in this deposition, including the names of her doctors, Nurse and Hinton, both highly respected gentlemen. Robert's denial of these accusations was essential, as there was no acceptable explanation for leaving his wife in this condition. An admission to any of Mary's accusations in this particular instance would have resulted in certain judgment against him. Robert, a highly skilled lawyer himself, would have weighed the plausibility of his denial and decided that in this case the judges might

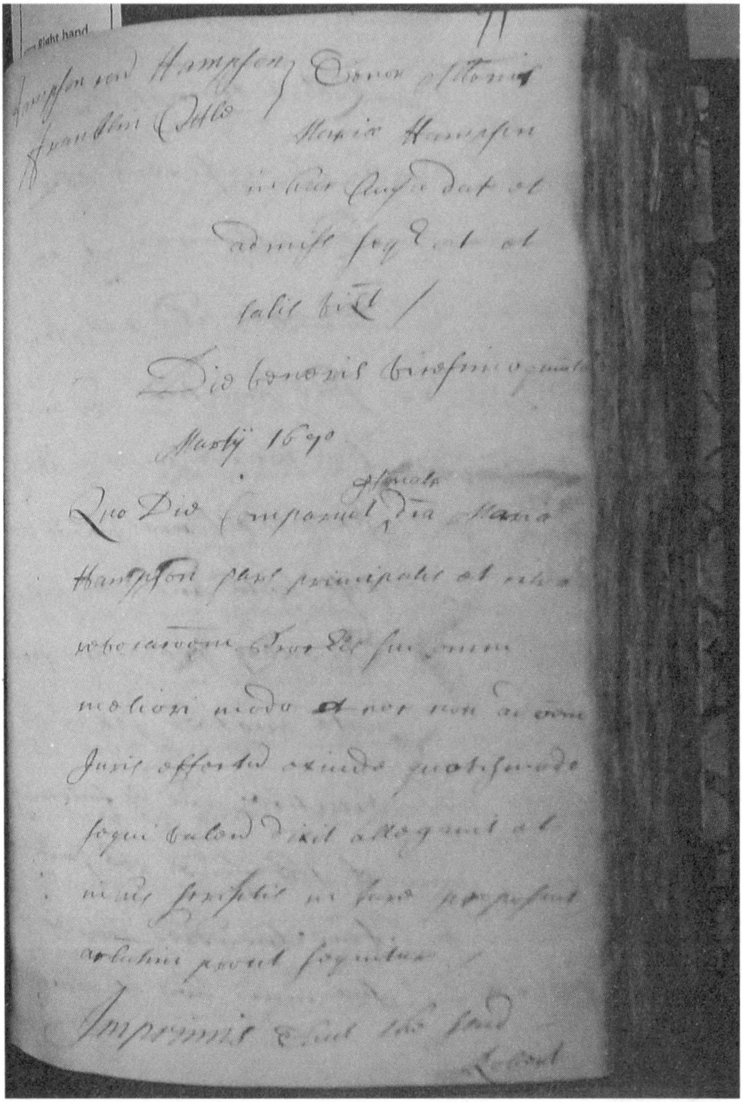

FIGURE 4. The first page of the legal record of Hampson v. Hampson, matrimonial cause: restoration of conjugal rights (1670) DEL1/110, High Court of Delegates. Printed by permission of the National Archives of the UK.

reasonably assume a pregnant woman's sore breast could be the result of her pregnancy and not of violence. Interestingly, in recounting other violent episodes Robert does not always resort to flat denial but rather seeks to portray his violent acts as the result of Mary's provocation, a strategy that many men in these types of cases employed.

All the narratives, both in the legal documents and in Mary's pamphlet, agree that Mary went to France in May 1664 for health reasons, leaving her young daughters Elizabeth (eight years old), Mary (three years old), and Anne (seven months old) with Robert. Elizabeth was sent to live with Robert's family at Taplow, while Mary and Anne were sent to Mary's Wingfield relatives in Keystone, Huntingdonshire. This distribution of the daughters reveals that in 1664 Robert was still quite keen to retain his connection with the Wingfield family despite his conflicts with Mary. Anne was still living with Dorothy Wingfield, Mary's aunt, when Mary returned to England in the spring of 1666. Elizabeth continued to live with Robert's unmarried sister, Katherine Hampson. The whereabouts of the daughter Mary at this time are unclear; She may have remained with her Wingfield relatives or joined her sister Elizabeth and her aunt Katherine.

Mary Hampson claims in her pamphlet that her mother, Elizabeth Wingfield, tried to convince Mary to live with her when Mary came back from France, rather than return to Robert. Mary refused to agree to her mother's wish and instead joined her husband in London. She adds that she came to regret this decision. In reality Mary had little choice but to return to Robert once back in England. Legally she could not live apart from him without the sanction of the church authorities, and she could obtain this sanction only if she proved that Robert refused to let her return to him. And even though Mary's pamphlet does not depict Robert as showing much enthusiasm to have his wife back, he realized there was little choice but to attempt a reconciliation. Of course, 1666 was not a particularly good year to return to London. The plague raged in the city throughout the summer, and in September the Great Fire destroyed much of the city, including Robert's chambers in the Inner Temple. The Hampsons also suffered an earlier personal tragedy that year when, in July 1666, the two-and-a-half-year-old Anne, along with her aunt Dorothy Wing-field, died in Huntingdonshire. They probably died of the plague, which had broken out in nearby Cambridge in June.[17] Anne's monument inscription is a rare instance of a moment of unity between Mary and Robert. It reads:

> Here lieth the body of Ann Hampson, the third daughter of Robert Hampson of the Inner Temple, London, esquire by Mary his wife the daughter and heir of Bodenham Wingfield who departed this life July the 16th 1666.[18]

In her Court of Arches testimony and later the High Court of Delegates testimony, Mary argued that her return to Robert's household was evidence that her stay in France was for health reasons and that he had given her permission to travel. By the time these court actions took place, it was imperative that she prove she did not go to France without Robert's permission. One wonders why this monument inscription, where Robert was willing to literally inscribe their relationship in stone, was never brought in as evidence of their renewed relationship that summer of 1666.

It may be that Mary simply chose not to discuss her dead child. Throughout the many narratives of the marriage, in the depositions and in print, there is little mention of the Hampson children. The infant Robert is never named by either Robert or Mary, but only alluded to by Robert when he states he had four children with Mary. The most extensive discussion of the children occurs in their case before the High Court of Delegates. Here Mary complains that after January 1668 Robert did not allow her to see her children.[19] As in many modern marital disputes, the children became pawns in the conflicts occurring in their parents' marriage. In the seventeenth century Robert had complete rights over his children, though as Mary's testimony shows, courts could see unreasonable separation between child and mother to be an act of cruelty. Robert took some pains to insist that Mary could not govern her children and that they were better off placed as they were. Unfortunately, Mary's daughters were never reconciled with their mother. Their resentment against her was fueled by Robert's version of their marital troubles, as will be discussed in Chapter Three.

Yet in the second half of 1666—despite plague, fire, and the death of their child—the court documents suggest there was a resumption of something like marital harmony in the Hampson household. Mary initially boarded with a family called Terry. Mary testified that sexual activity between the couple resumed, and that she even believed herself to be pregnant in the autumn of 1666. Later Robert would testify that Mary refused to have sex with him, though the exact timing of this refusal is unclear. Mary states that on one occasion she did refuse to have sex with her husband, but when she explained to him that she was in the "manner of women," or menstruating, Robert was quite happy to accept her refusal.[20] This frank discussion of the couple's sexual activities in their court testimony was important because it helped establish that there was a full resumption of marital relations after Mary returned from France. Only by convincing the judges that Robert accepted her back into his house and bed could Mary hope the judges would require Robert to continue to maintain her financially. Robert's strategy in his court testimony, on the other hand, was to prove that she was ineligible for support because she refused to carry out her responsibilities as a wife. He attempted to undermine her claim to financial support by asserting she had betrayed the marriage in so many ways that she could not possibly have any claim to alimony from him.

These court battles were, however, in the future. From April 1666 until January 1668, the couple lived together quietly, first lodging in the Terry household and later in Robert's rebuilt chambers in the Inner Temple. It appears this was also a period of financial calm and professional advancement for Robert. He sat on a number of committees in the Inner Temple and was commissioned to rebuild chambers in the Inner Temple that had been destroyed by the Great Fire, and to collect the rent from them. He sold one of these chambers to the Fen Office, the administrative body that continued to oversee the Bedford Levels or fenland project. In his personal life, he and Mary were getting along, and Mary may have been pregnant again.

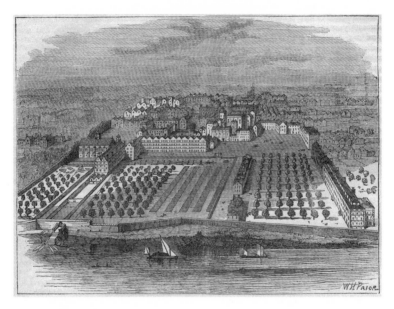

FIGURE 5. The Inner Temple, an engraving by W. H. Prior, after an original in the Inner Temple Library (c. 1671) in *London Old and New* (London, 1878). Author's collection.

The only unusual event recorded from this period was no doubt seen as odd but inconsequential at the time. (Unfortunately for Mary, it was to take on a much more sinister aspect in the couple's later marital disputes.) This was the incident of the Italian and his tale of poisoned kisses. Mary told the judges in her testimony in both court cases that an Italian lodged with the Terry family at the same time she and Robert had rooms there. She states in her depositions that one day this Italian told her he knew a way to poison a person with a kiss. Mary told the judges she informed Robert of this story in order to warn him that the Italian could be dangerous.

Robert later told the judges that Mary said this to threaten him. Popular literature at the time often portrayed poison as the choice of weapon for murderous wives, and stereotypically, Italians. Whether Mary told Robert of the Italian's claim as a warning, a threat, or simply as information, it was to be particularly damaging to Mary later. In both court cases, Mary was forced to answer accusations that she had threatened to poison her husband, though it is clear the judges accepted her version of the events. If the judges had believed Mary intended to poison Robert, they would have released him from all obligations toward Mary and possibly imprisoned her. No doubt this was the reason Robert introduced this particular accusation into the proceedings.

Robert also claimed that Mary attempted to stab him. This accusation too began from a minor, if more clearly violent, episode in the Hampson marriage after Mary's return from France. In her pamphlet, Mary recalls this incident rather disingenuously, claiming that although Robert accused her of drawing a "pen-knife through his hand and cut his finger" and scratching "him in the face," she had "answered all this to Mr. Hampson's shame." This statement suggests that Robert lied about the incident. And though Robert certainly attempted to make the most of this incident in his testimony, Mary admits in both her depositions that the incident with the pen-knife took place, though she plays down its significance. She explains in her court testimony how one morning while she was using a pen-knife to scrape or sharpen a pencil, Robert came into the chamber speaking "harsh words to her" and tried to take the pen-knife out of her hand. Mary goes on to explain that, fearing her husband's anger and what he might do if he had the knife, she "kept the said penknife from him." At this point she describes how he "laid hold upon the blade and thereby and by his own willfulness" cut his own hand.[21] It is clear in Mary's deposition that she was answering an accusation levied against her by Robert. Unfortunately there is no record of Robert's version of this episode in the surviving court records.

The incident with the pen-knife was only part of a much larger dispute that lasted for four days in January 1668 and escalated dangerously. It is difficult to ascertain the exact chronology of events over the days of the conflict. The pen-knife incident probably occurred after the conflict had begun, because in Mary's version of events Robert was already in a "passion." The subject of this conflict was Robert's desire to sell property that was part of her second jointure. He could sell any property that was his, whether it was in a jointure or not,[22] but it appears in this case that the buyer was unwilling to risk the possibility of costly legal action in the future and instead asked for Mary's agreement before he would buy the property. Mary's refusal to give her permission for the sale of the land enraged Robert because he believed he had secured a good price on the land and could invest the money elsewhere for greater profit. Mary's refusal was based on her suspicions of Robert's financial judgment and her very real concern that should he die she would be left with little to support herself and her children. The disagreement over this sale of property quickly escalated into violence on both sides.

Robert claims in his court testimony that one morning Mary "came out of her bed in her smock into another room" and proceeded to pull his hair, spit in his face, and call him "rascal, cheat, knave, and villain and such like base language without any just cause given." He admits that after this attack he responded by kicking her in the "buttocks" and calling her "slut and jade" and threatened to withhold meat and drink from her. Mary's version of events is not very different, except she justifies her actions. She relates in her testimony that one morning Robert came to her bedchamber and forced her to get up, all the time using "provoking words" and threatening to call the officers of the Inner Temple to throw her out of the house. Mary claims she was so afraid he would "maim and mischief" her that "for her own defense and to save herself . . . she did lay hold on her said husband's hair and pull him thereby, but did not hurt him or pluck any of his hair off his head." Interestingly, in her pamphlet Mary recalls that she was accused of scratching Robert in this episode rather than pulling his hair. There is no mention of scratching in Mary or Robert's court testimony.[23]

This altercation came after another unpleasant incident that appears to have aggravated the dispute over the jointure land. Robert, hoping to intimidate or convince Mary to agree to his wishes, had arranged for his friends to come to the house and talk with her. As discussed earlier, the intervention of friends and neighbors in order to mediate conflicts between married couples was seen not only as socially acceptable but as the duty of the community. In a perversion of this practice, Robert invited his friends Richard Powell and his wife and Hopton Shuter to supper in order to pressure Mary to agree to Robert's demands to sign away her jointure rights to the property in question. Both Shuter and Powell were members of the Inner Temple and close friends and colleagues of Robert. In her pamphlet, Mary recounts the supper in vivid detail, where she accuses Shuter of saying he would make a "spread-eagle" of her and send her to Bedlam, a brutal institution for the mad. Mary's court testimony is less colorful, accusing Shuter of speaking to her in a "cruel and base manner" at Robert's instigation. Robert does not comment on this dinner party specifically in his depositions, but he does claim that at some point during this conflict she was so out of control that he was forced to call the chaplain of the Inner Temple church, Dr. Ball, to speak with her; according to Robert, she responded with "slighting and abusing words."[24]

These events finally reached their most dangerous point one or two nights after the supper party. In her pamphlet Mary describes how Robert threatened her with a pistol, and that he admitted to this action in his Court of Arches deposition. There is no record of Mary's testimony about this incident in the Count of Arches case, but Robert's admission is recorded. He remarks that Mary was so "insolent and furious against him" that he was forced to protect himself by showing "her a pistol, but there was neither powder nor bullet in the said pistol." In his High Court of Delegates testimony Robert again asserts that he only "showed" Mary the pistol to bring her into submission, and that there was no powder or bullet in it.[25]

Mary's version of events in her High Court of Delegates deposition attests to a more terrifying encounter. In this deposition she claims that despite Robert's cruel treatment during those days she remained with him out of her "love to him." In her pamphlet she says she came to him at about eleven o'clock in the evening in order to talk. In her court testimony, she describes how he responded to her by pulling out "a pistol which was charged with powder and bullet and putt the same to her breast threatening and intending to shoot her there in a furious and angry manner to the great terror and disquiet" of Mary.[26] In her pamphlet she describes how she and her maid fled the house in the night, and that a reconciliation was later brokered by Mary's attorney and relative, Serjeant at Law John Fountaine.

Neither Mary nor Robert comes out of this conflict particularly well. Mary clearly plays down her own violent responses in her pamphlet, while trying to justify them in her court testimony. She understood that in her culture any violent response from a woman would be condemned. What is striking in the testimony of both Mary and Robert is their willingness to admit to violent acts carried out privately and without witnesses, albeit clothed in justification. It may be that both were drawing on cultural perceptions of just anger, each hoping the court would view his or her actions as the reasonable and even necessary response to the aggression and injustice of the other.[27]

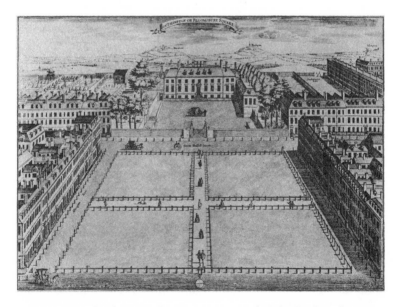

FIGURE 6. New Southampton Square, an engraving by John Bowles, after an original work by Sutton Nicholls (c. 1670) in *A History of the Squares of London* (London 1907). Author's collection.

After the events of January 1668, the couple began their last attempt at marital cohabitation. Mary and Robert appear to have been committed to putting their past conflicts behind them. They attempted to live together peacefully and reestablish themselves in the gentry community. Robert was even willing to make some financial investment for this purpose. The couple took a house in the fashionable New Southampton Square, now Bloomsbury Square. This area was, in 1720, described as being spacious, with good houses and inhabited by the gentry.[28] In addition to terraced houses, the area boasted the London homes of several noblemen, including the Earls of Southampton, Thanet, and Chesterfield as well as the Duke of Bedford.

However, even at the outset there were some troubling indications that this reconciliation would be no more successful than earlier ones. It appears that during this time Robert was actively attempting to turn Mary's mother against Mary in the hopes that Elizabeth Wingfield would disinherit Mary and leave all her property to him. Mary says in her pamphlet that Elizabeth had been encouraged by the lawyer John Fountaine to make a will setting up a trust for Mary in order to keep all of Elizabeth's property out of Robert's hands and provide Mary with an income. Mary believed her mother had made such a trust.

Mary also records that her relationship with her mother was not particularly good in the two years before Elizabeth's death. She explains in her pamphlet that this was because Elizabeth was overly emotional or even hysterical during their visits—as Mary puts it, she suffered from "fits of the mother." According to Mary, Robert feared that this was dangerous to Mary and did not allow her to visit Elizabeth. It is also possible that Mary was pregnant at some point during this time. It was believed that pregnant women were especially vulnerable to "fits of the mother." Mary's claim that she was often ill during this time suggests it, though she does not mention pregnancy as a reason for her estrangement with her mother.

Instead, in this testimony Mary blames Robert for coming between her mother and herself with a variety of lies, among them that she continued to behave badly toward Robert and that she had converted to Roman Catholicism, of which Elizabeth heartily disapproved. Mary explains in her court depositions that she did not visit her mother "for some time till she might have opportunity to clear herself of that falsity" of being a Roman Catholic.[29] She also claims that at the end of her mother's life the two women were reconciled.

Whatever the truth about Mary and Elizabeth's relationship, Robert was able to manipulate the situation in such a way as to ensure that he got hold of all of Elizabeth's land and much of her personal property after her death. He did this through the legal device of a nuncupative will. It was proved, or validated, in the Consistory Court of Canterbury where a short transcription of it can still be read:

> Memorandum: That on or about the second day of September in the year of our lord God one thousand six hundred and sixty nine Elizabeth Wingfield of St. Clement's Danes in the County of Middlesex widow being sick of the [illness] of which she died but of perfect mind and memory with a serious intent to make her last will and testament non-cupative she spake these words or the like in effect viz.: "all the estate that she had in the world she gave to her son in law Mr. Robert Hampson" in the presence of credible witnesses—George Wotten and Johanna Dickerson.[30]

The validity of a nuncupative (or by-voice) will was based on the presence of two credible witnesses. Mary maintains in her pamphlet that Wotten and Dickerson were not credible, and that they had financial motives for signing this statement because Robert owed Wotten money, and Dickerson was a young woman of "no repute," inferring she was paid for the job and of questionable morals. Non-cupative wills were not uncommon, but they were vulnerable to legal challenge, and yet no one lodged a legal challenge to this will on Mary's behalf in court. Because there were no legal challenges, it was approved quite quickly, and Robert began selling off Elizabeth Wingfield's property, as a deed of sale to Martin Buck in 1670 proves.[31] Mary was able to secure some of her mother's property, however. In the court documents, Robert accuses Mary of keeping some of Elizabeth's jewelry, money, and documents away from him.

After Elizabeth Wingfield's death, Robert had no financial reason to continue living with Mary, and sometime in December 1669 or January 1670 he moved out of the New Southampton Square house and into lodgings in Exeter House, abandoning Mary. He refused to provide her with any financial support, and in retaliation she began to sell off a variety of household items. Because Mary feared leaving in case Robert should lock the house against her, she sent her servant, Katherine Browne, to the pawn broker to sell household items. Unfortunately, Katherine was to pay a high price for following Mary's instructions. On discovering that items were being sold, Robert sent for Katherine to be arrested, as legally all the items in the house were his.

Mary may also have asked a man named Sillyard to help her sell these items. She met him months earlier when he came to ask about renting rooms in the New Southampton Square house. Mary wrote in her pamphlet that Robert agreed to rent the house on the condition that they take in lodgers. She states in her court testimony that Sillyard came to look at the rooms but chose not to take them because they were too expensive. She also said that Sillyard returned to the house once, but she refused to allow him in and told him she "wished him to forbear coming to her house."[32] Apparently Sillyard went away at that time, but he also left behind a letter, which Mary gave to Robert. Sillyard does not appear again in the Hampsons' court testimony or Mary's pamphlet until the night of Katherine Browne's arrest.

That night, Robert recalls in his court testimony that he and his friend Henry Poulton went to the house of the justice of the peace after having accused both Katherine and Mary of selling Robert's household goods. At the justice's house, they were met by a servant, who told them Sillyard was inside the house with the justice and was threatening him. Mary and Katherine were also in the justice's house by that time. Robert and Poulton entered and began arguing with Sillyard. Next, according to his deposition, Robert took out the letter that Sillyard had written to

Mary many months before and claimed that "the said Mary being conscious of the naughtiness thereof suddenly snatched the same of the said justice's hands and tore it which affront enraged the justice."[33] Throughout this episode Robert refers to Sillyard as Mary's "gallant" or lover. Mary begins her account by stating "that she is innocent and not guilty of any wanton dalliance with the said Sillyard and doth believe that her said husband doth himself, in his conscience, think her innocent and not guilty of any ill behaviour with the said Sillyard."[34] However, Mary does not contradict Robert about the presence of Sillyard that evening. She also admits that in her anger she took the letter "out of the said justice's hand and rent it in pieces."[35] And yet, although Mary's response suggests the letter was incriminating, apparently it was not. Mary actually kept the pieces of the letter and offered them to the High Court of Delegates in the expectation that, as she states, the letter "will justify her"—which it did. The judges did not accept Robert's accusations of adultery.[36]

This incident brings up some interesting questions. Why were Sillyard and Mary at the justice's house at the same time, if they simply had a passing acquaintance? Why is there no mention of Sillyard in Mary's pamphlet? Two explanations come to mind. The first was that Sillyard was a plant hired by Robert to impugn Mary's good name; in her court testimony Mary insinuates as much. There is a Thomas Sillyard listed as having rooms in the Inner Temple at the same time Robert Hampson lived there.[37] Other marital discord pamphlets in this period suggest this strategy was not uncommon.[38] In the pamphlet published by Tobias Cage, Tobias claimed his wife Mary introduced a woman of ill repute into his house so she could accuse him of having a mistress.[39] Interestingly, he says in his pamphlet that Mary Cage's lawyer was Richard Powell. Mary mentions him in her pamphlet as one who supported Robert in his abusive behavior toward her. Powell may have suggested to Robert that he introduce Sillyard into his household, as he had earlier suggested Mary Cage introduce the maid who accused Tobias Cage of sexual impropriety.

However, it is more likely that Sillyard's acquaintance with Mary has a less dramatic explanation. It looks as if Mary did continue to have some contact with Sillyard. Several times in her pamphlet she describes seeking the help of men in business matters. Sillyard may have offered to carry some of Mary's household goods to the pawn broker, just as Katherine, Mary's servant, did. This would explain why Katherine, Sillyard, and Mary were all called before the justice of the peace that night. Mary explains in her depositions that the night she was summoned to the justice she feared she would be sent to prison. She also describes how she defended the maid. Unfortunately, though Mary and Sillyard apparently escaped imprisonment, Katherine was sent to Bridewell, a brutal prison of correction for women.

Shortly before Katherine's arrest and Mary's summons to the justice of the peace, Robert managed to lock Mary out of the New Southampton Square house. Mary recalled how he had a servant boy trick her into leaving the house by telling her one of her neighbors was ill and was asking for her company. Once Mary was out of the house, Robert and several other men entered and later refused to let Mary return. She found herself in the street with literally nothing but the clothes on her back. The fact that Robert believed he could treat his wife in this way, with little worry about repercussions to his finances and professional reputation, speaks volumes for the vulnerability of married women in seventeenth-century society. There are many examples in this period of men violently removing their wives from the family home and refusing to allow them to return. For example, in 1602 Elizabeth Garth complained in a court action filed with the Court of Requests[40] that her husband, Robert Garth, "moste unkindelie" sent her "from his house with onelie tenn shillings in her purse, or therabouts, & a paier of hose or shoes scarse worth the wearinge."[41] Margaret Cunningham recalls in her memoir that in 1604 her husband, Sir James Hamilton, "cruellie, in the night, put both her [her maid] and me forth of his house naked [in only their night shifts] and would not suffer us to put on our cloaths."[42] In 1718, John Walton forced his wife and her children (from an earlier marriage) out of the house with a horsewhip in threatening that she "and her Kitlings . . . shou'd never come there or into . . . [his] house again."[43] Mary Hampson was right to fear leaving her New Southampton Square house in case she, like many women of her time, found herself similarly homeless.

Mary describes in her later court testimony that Robert kept her clothes, the money her mother had given her, family heirlooms, and other items. The only property Mary managed to retain were those things she had kept elsewhere.[44] Robert's testimony agrees for the most part with her description of events. In his own testimony, he admits he came to the house with several people, "one of which had a sword which he usually wears." He continued, saying that finding Mary gone he entered the house and refused to admit her when she returned because he had "reason for the same," or good reason to refuse to allow Mary back in the house—though he does not explain what that reason was. He admits he broke into her "boxes, chests, trunks, and desk" in the house and found ninety-five pounds of gold and forty to fifty shillings in silver and "nothing else." He also includes an interesting detail, claiming that he found some pictures "the said Mary had drawn which pictures he hath returned to the said Mary." This comment suggests Mary was an amateur artist. Robert's brother-in-law, the painter Edmund Ashfield,[45] lived near the Hampsons, and it is intriguing to consider that Mary may have taken lessons from him. The question of why Robert felt it important to return the drawings to Mary and to testify to this in court is also interesting. In a court case between Robert and Elizabeth Moulton, Elizabeth was allowed to keep a needlework cushion "which she herself wrought at a boarding school before her intermarriage."[46] It seems there was a cultural expectation that material produced by a woman's hands was in some fundamental way the property of the woman. Finally, Robert justified the confiscation of Mary's goods and money by claiming he believed the property was his—and certainly all the property was legally his under coverture. Mary's testimony reveals she either did not understand the extent of the legal repercussions of coverture or believed the judges would follow the customary practice that accepted women had some moral (though not legal) claim to property they brought to the household.

Mary's whereabouts following her eviction from her home are not known. However, what is certain is that within weeks of being locked out of the house, she brought her case to the ecclesiastical Court of Arches. The testimony from this case and the subsequent appeal to the High Court of Delegates provides many intriguing details and contradictions in the Hampsons' long and tortuous marital disputes that are missing in the account Mary eventually published. The court testimony also shows now the experiences of individuals were shaped by customary practice. Many of the strategies Mary and Robert employed in their testimony built on cultural norms and expectations. Much of the surviving material related to cases of marital conflict in the seventeenth century reveals that spouses often accused one another of Roman Catholic sympathies, as Robert accuses Mary. Women were often accused of having lovers or gallants. Men were accused of beating their wives—especially on the breasts, genitals, and buttocks. Men were also accused of mistreatment and neglect of their wives during pregnancy, of locking women out of their homes, and of imprisoning them within their homes. Accusations of men starving their wives are also common. Women were accused of shrewish tongues, withholding sexual access, and spending money irresponsibly. Women were also accused of selling household goods without their husband's permission. All of this is not to say that couples involved in marital disputes made up, or lied about, the events that took place in their marriage (though at times this is clearly the case). Instead it shows how the acts of individuals were shaped and motivated by cultural attitudes and norms, and the narration of these acts was further influenced by these attitudes and norms.

And yet, despite the cultural shaping of Mary and Robert's testimony, this testimony shows they agreed on the core facts of their marriage. They both agreed that Robert beat Mary. They agreed that he included mortgaged property in the jointure he settled upon her at their marriage. They agreed that he took possession of goods and land belonging to both Mary and her mother. They agreed that he kept Mary's children from her. And they agreed that he threw her out of their house and refused to pay maintenance to her. Robert admits to all of this in his testimony, though he defends the less socially acceptable of these actions. But did he pay servants and others to betray Mary? Did he carry wild tales of her Roman Catholic conversion to Elizabeth Wingfield? Did he actually try to kill Mary? These accusations lack the evidence needed for accepting them as certain. Mary, for her part, admitted to having a sharp tongue. She told others of Robert's violent actions and financial dishonesty long after the events had occurred and a reconciliation was achieved, thus damaging his reputation. She stole documents out of Robert's study, and she sold household goods without permission. But was she an adulteress? Did she threaten to poison Robert? Did she abandon him and go to France without permission in 1664? Again, there is little evidence for these accusations. The ruling in favor of Mary in the Court of Arches case and the settlement made in the High Court of Delegates is strong evidence that the judges did not accept the more serious accusations levied against Mary by Robert. However, the relatively modest maintenance he was expected to pay suggests they were not convinced that she was a particularly dutiful wife by the standards of the time. Instead the judges, no doubt wearily, accepted that this couple could not live together and allowed them to live apart legally, with Robert charged with providing a modest maintenance of £100 per year for Mary.

Painful as their marital conflicts were up to 1670, the course of Mary and Robert's disputes and their separation followed the tired and trodden paths of many failed early modern marriages. Small conflicts developed into larger ones, which usually included issues related to money, episodes of neglect, some form of physical violence, abandonment, and finally actions in the courts. It is in the afterlife of the Hampson marriage, as shown in legal and other documents, where the Hampsons' behavior veers far from the norm. After the action in the High Court of Delegates was resolved through mutual agreement, Robert and Mary attempted to retreat into their own lives, but their financial needs as well as their anger and resentment continued to bring them together such that the separate lives both attempted to build were constantly destabilized.

Chapter 2

AFTERLIFE *of a* MARRIAGE

Accusations and Recriminations

In the years that followed Mary and Robert's legal separation, the couple continued to be locked in a cycle of conflict over the payment of Mary's alimony. Her attempts to collect her alimony, and his violent determination to pay her nothing, had unintended consequences for them both. Mary continued to petition the High Court of Delegates to force Robert to pay, while he claimed more and more widely that she was dead and increasingly used violence in his attempts not to pay—including beating a gentleman acting on Mary's behalf, and having her thrown among a mob. She also believed that he hired the notorious spy Edmund Everard to follow and threaten her. She finally felt compelled to put her story in print, and Robert responded with his own pamphlet. At the time of his death, his reputation and finances were in tatters, while Mary lingered on in poverty. Many of the details of these later years come from her pamphlet, but other pamphlets, court documents, and letters add many details not found in the published story. These create an even richer, if somewhat more complicated, picture of the Hampsons' life in the aftermath of their marriage.

After coming to an agreement in the Hampsons' High Court of Delegates case in May 1671, Mary traveled to France almost immediately. She explains in a letter to the eminent lawyer and later ambassador Sir William Trumbull why she chose to leave England:

> I [live] in a strange country, for if it be possible I would not live in England where my husband by his false reports hath so stained my repu-

tation that I think it not safe for me to live there, for what ever affront is put upon me I find no justice therefore I desire to live where I am judged by my life and conversation and not by the report of a second Mahomet whom would do as the first did, destroy me.[1]

Despite the fact that the Court of Arches and the High Court of Delegates upheld Mary's rights as Robert Hampson's wife, her reputation was irreparably harmed within the gentry community. This made life in England uncomfortable at best and treacherous at worst. In France, and later the Netherlands, Mary tried to live quietly as a respectable, if impoverished, English gentlewoman. Two sources agree that she resumed using her maiden name of Wingfield when she began her new life in France. Francis Burke, a London merchant who acted for her on business matters, would testify in a later court action that Mary called herself Wingfield in France because it was the custom there "for women though married to write their maiden names."[2] She was also identified as "Mrs Wingfield alias Hampson" in a pamphlet published in 1679.[3]

Mary tells us that after her separation from Robert she lodged in the house of a Mademoiselle de La Porte in Paris. Here she was likely serving as a type of gentlewoman servant, a position for which she was well suited given her family status, her education, and her fluent French. Gentlewomen servants during this period served as companions, engaging in household activities with the mistress of the house such as sewing, reading, and the like. They might also run errands and oversee the servants in housekeeping matters. This position in the household of an aristocratic French woman would not be seen as demeaning and would have allowed Mary to form useful social connections. It is also interesting to note that, though during her first stay in France in 1664–1666 she attached herself to the Protestant English community in Paris, in the 1670s she was living among the Catholic French aristocracy. This can be seen as a further attempt to put distance between herself and the English gentry in order to create a new life as the modest gentlewoman Mrs. Wingfield rather than the defamed Mrs. Hampson. In this she was initially successful. She refers to the help given to her by Mademoiselle de La Porte and Anne Geneviève, the Duchess of Longueville. She also received help from a woman she does not name but refers to as a "person of quality" who was the wife of her lawyer in Paris. By 1673 Mary appears to have become established in the French aristocratic community in Paris, though at a very humble level.

Unfortunately, Mary's financial position was precarious. Whatever of value she had managed to keep from Robert could only have provided for her immediate needs. For Mary, and other women in her position in the seventeenth century, being awarded alimony was one thing; actually forcing the spouse to pay it was quite another. Mary complains bitterly at the end of the second edition of her printed story that "for as it doth appear there is no penalty against Mr. Hampson but excommunication; where he suffers and stands excommunicated, and I have not bread to live on." Quickly Mary learned that her new life in France as Mrs. Wingfield in the household of Mademoiselle de La Porte was not going to be as easy to maintain as she had hoped, given Robert's refusal to pay the alimony according to the terms of their agreement.

Mary's frustration with the ineffectiveness of the English Church to enforce its judgments was shared by many. In the late seventeenth century, excommunication, or the banning of an individual from attending church, had lost its sting. People were willing to put up with this ban for a long period of time, especially if the person's host community was not concerned by the ban.[4] Robert Hampson's associates in the Inner Temple were not interested in the fact that he had been excommunicated. Throughout the 1670s, he held a variety of offices and sat on many committees in the Inner Temple. He was awarded building contracts, mediated disputes, and generally was very involved in the management of the Inner Temple community. He also continued to serve as a circuit judge and in 1680 was made a serjeant of law, a senior order of barristers from which common law judges were chosen.[5] His state of excommunication was completely overlooked in his professional life. Nor does his refusal to pay alimony appear to have concerned any of his professional colleagues or social acquaintances. Mary was right to be frustrated at the inability of the church court to enforce alimony payments; they simply had very little power in the late seventeenth century.[6] She could have taken the matter to another court, but this would have involved expensive legal fees she could not afford.

Mary's choice to live in France also complicated matters. She claims in her pamphlet that soon after her arrival in France she received a letter from Sir John Fiennes, who warned her that Robert Hampson was spreading rumors she had died. Sometime later, when Fiennes took affidavits to Robert affirming that Mary was alive, Robert beat the old gentleman, according to Mary in her pamphlet. And although there is no independent evidence of the beating, there is evidence that Robert refused to acknowledge that Mary was alive and was quite ready to evade the efforts of those who agreed to help her. The merchant Francis Burke discovered the lengths to which Robert would go to avoid paying alimony when he attempted to collect this money for Mary.

In Burke's 1684 testimony to the High Court of Delegates (the court that continued to have jurisdiction over the details of the Hampson marriage agreement), Burke describes Robert's unwillingness to pay the alimony he had agreed to and was morally obliged to pay. Burke explains how over an eighteen-month period he attempted to collect Mary's alimony but was consistently refused by Robert on the flimsiest of excuses. Initially, Burke explains, Robert "took exception" to the procuration, or the bill she had prepared, "pleading it was not sufficient and said he would not nor did he pay any money" to Burke. Burke was certainly a persistent man, sending to Mary asking for another bill from Paris. This time, she sent a document with, as Burke testifies, "the names of several other persons [including] Mr. Daniel Arthur an eminent merchant and a person being one of them whose character and manner" Burke "well knoweth." This time Robert refused to accept the document because it was in French. Burke had it translated and returned again to speak with Robert and did "show unto him [Robert] the original procuration in French and delivered unto him the translation there of in English, which he [Robert] looked upon and read." Burke then recounts that Robert said he had to "go out of town and should return about six weeks to come and that he [Robert] would consider of it"—that is, he would consider paying Mary her money when he returned. Burke waited the six weeks and then went to Robert's chambers in the Inner Temple, only to be told he was not in London. Three weeks later, Burke went again to the chambers and managed to speak to Robert, who refused to pay any money "until he was better satisfied." The exhausted Burke told all this to the judges (or delegates) of the High Court of Delegates, Thomas Exton and Thomas Pinfold, and also provided the bills as evidence.[7]

Four years earlier, in 1680, Mary entered into a correspondence with Sir William Trumbull in an attempt to gain his help in securing her alimony.[8] There is a rawness in these letters that makes Mary's frustration and anger easy to see, and it is unlike the calm and assured narrative voice she uses in her pamphlet or the respectful, if at times pitiful, tone found in her court testimony. One can also hear her growing desperation, which even Trumbull recognized and acknowledged in a note he wrote on one of the letters.

Mary's first letter to Trumbull, dated August 9, 1680, opens by acknowledging some previous assistance he had provided and uses this to excuse her boldness in asking for further help:

> The compassion you was pleased to show me in my business gives me the confidence to beg the favor of you to let me know if Mr. Hampson hath paid the fifty pounds the last day of July as was ordered to Mr. Franklin and likewise what way I must take to oblige Mr. Hampson to pay me my alimony.

In this letter she also claims that she feared Robert intended to kill her. She tells Trumbull about a recent event near the Inner Temple, when Robert had his clerk throw her out into the street and cry out to passers-by that she was a madwoman, "the last June having escaped Mr. Hampson's hands I had liked to have been killed by the rabble under the notion that I was a mad woman."[9] In her next letter, dated October 20, she again refers to this incident, explaining to Trumbull that this experience had made her so fearful and angry that she left England soon afterward without taking care of her financial affairs: "I was in so great [a] passion too be out of the place where I had received such barbarous treatment that I gave no order in my business." It is in this letter that she suggests she might write the story of her sufferings and have it published—which she later did. It is also in this letter that she calls Robert Hampson a "monster of ingratitude." (The term *monster* was often used to describe abusive husbands.[10]) In subsequent letters, interspersed with matters of business, she continues to reveal her frustration and her fear. She tells Trumbull that nothing she does can "assuage his [Robert's] malice." She pleads with Trumbull to tell her in "what manner I may proceed for I can no longer live as a slave." She explains poignantly that for more than a decade she has pursued Robert in order to enforce the agreement they both freely entered into and is now so "out of patience that I can have no rest for I cannot live in England upon so small a sum yearly nor here unless it be well and quarterly paid."

As the letters continue into 1681, Mary becomes increasingly despondent. She admits to Trumbull that "I see Mr. Hampson will never pay me as the agreement obliges him." In her last letter to Trumbull, she alludes to her own death, telling him that "I would have a little rest before I go hence and be no more seen [dies]. I employ persons of several judgments to find where is the faithful man that is a lover of truth and justice." This echoes an earlier letter where she wrote, "I hope still that God will not harden all men's harts and that some will seek to do me justice, his will be done." Trumbull was moved by Mary's letters. On her last letter to him he writes a message to a T.R.[11] asking this person to give Mary Hampson assistance, explaining that "Nor could I bethink myself of a person more fit to do this than thyself whom I know to be a lover of justice and a friend of oppressed persons."[12] It is unclear whether this letter, and its message to "T.R.," was ever forwarded. As the Burke testimony shows, Mary continued to pursue Robert for her alimony for many years, with little success.

These letters add detail and pathos to Mary's published account of her long struggle to secure her alimony. However, the letters also describe one intriguing detail that is not present in her printed account, nor in any other document. In her letter dated April 4, 1681, she assures Trumbull that:

> This gentleman whom does me the kindness too bring this letter to your hand can testify that I am Mrs. Hampson he having seen me with my husband that was in England. I say that was for I am well informed that he [Robert] is and hath been married a considerable time to another by which I am free before God. But I know it will be hard for too prove it, neither should I desire it for I seek not his life, but would be free before the world [as] I am before God.

Here Mary is accusing Robert of remarrying and thus being involved in an illegal relationship with another woman. This was no small accusation. In 1604 bigamy was made a felony punishable by death. And while most men (and some women) who were accused of this crime received a milder punishment—often branding on the hand—others were executed.[13] However, given Robert Hampson's status as a sergeant at law and a respected lawyer, it is unlikely he ever went through a marriage ceremony with another woman. It is, though, very possible he kept a mistress, which was morally questionable but socially accepted for men in situations like Robert's. Still, it is possible that Robert might have been tempted to marry again if the woman brought money to the marriage. If he had been foolish enough to actually marry another woman, he would have had an even greater motivation for spreading rumors of Mary's death than simply to avoid his alimony payments.

There is evidence that even if Robert was not plotting to kill Mary, he was actively spreading rumors and even swearing in court documents that she was dead. This had one unintended consequence for him, however. Mary had inherited property in Huntingdonshire when her uncle, John Whalley, died in 1664, as has been discussed in Chapter One. This property was rented out and brought in an annual income of about a hundred pounds. The money went to Robert because even though they were separated he still had the right to all of her income (though he was expected to pay her alimony). By claiming she was dead, Robert apparently did not realize he would lose some of the income from this property.[14] According to Whalley's will, after Mary's death her daughters were to inherit the property, with the daughter Elizabeth receiving the largest portion and the two daughters Mary and Anne receiving smaller portions. In addition, according to the will, even though Elizabeth could leave her portion of the property to her children, the property that went to Mary and Anne had to return to Whalley's nephew and his heirs when Mary and Anne died (this was probably an error in the writing of the will). Anne died in 1666, so according to Whalley's will (of 1664) the income from the property that would come to Anne in the case of Mary Hampson's death should by the terms of the will have returned to Whalley's nephew. Robert Hampson took the nephew to court in 1674 in order to rectify what he believed to be the error in the will. He claims this was to protect the rights of his daughters, though as his daughters' guardian he would have had control of the rental income from the property. Robert was apparently successful in arguing that the portion left to his daughters Mary and Anne should descend to them and their heirs; in this case Elizabeth and Mary would have inherited Anne's portion of the property if their mother had actually been dead. In the testimony from this court action, Robert is recorded as swearing that Mary was dead when he knew full well she was alive.[15]

Mary also came to believe that Robert had employed a man to watch her, and even to kill her. This man was Edmund Everard, one of the most notorious government informers of the late seventeenth century. Mary met Everard in 1671, with disastrous consequences for her, though she fared better than many of his victims. Everard was a con man who used whatever knowledge he gained and his extraordinary ability to construct false tales in order to extort money and place himself in a position of power over others. There was also something pathological about him; at times his schemes put his own life in danger. When he met Mary, he appears to have been a small-time confidence trickster. She describes in her pamphlet their ill-fated meeting when she first arrived in Paris after her rapid departure from England in May 1671 at the end of the High Court of Delegates case. She says she met "two old Irish men" on the boat from England who then also joined the coach to Paris. These men accompanied Mary to a lodging house in Paris. She recalls in her pamphlet:

> The next evening after I came to Paris, the mistress of the house desired I would come and sup in the hall, assuring me there was only my two country men, (as she named them) and a young man of their acquaintance. I did go down and after supper, one of the men told me the young man's name was Everard a kinsman of his. The said Mr. Everard addressed himself to me, telling me he had a great desire to render all the service his poor condition would admit of to all English.

Everard's willingness to serve should have made her suspicious, but Mary was in a difficult position, unwilling to show herself in the city until she was properly dressed and could present herself as a gentlewoman. She employed Everard on some small errands, and he, true to his practice, was not particularly honest in these dealings. For example, he stole money she gave him to redeem her watch from a pawnbroker. This petty larceny was only the beginning of Everard's abuse of Mary. Unfortunately, she must have confided in Everard about her marital situation and the wrongs she had suffered. Later she would complain that he was one of the "instruments" Robert used against her, but it seems she gave Everard the information he needed to make use of her situation for his gain. She was never discreet about Robert's treatment of her; in her earlier court depositions, she admitted angering Robert by telling people in Huntingdon about his mistreatment. Unfortunately, Everard used the information she gave him to advance his own interests at the cost of hers.

It is unclear when (or even if) Everard became acquainted with Robert. Everard claimed in a pamphlet he wrote in 1679 that Robert, or as he names him, "Mr Hampton and the Lady Anne Gordon . . . would have me vindicate [them] against some other of their rivals," which Everard "promise[d] them I would do, to better insinuate myself into their secrets."[16] This statement does not exactly indicate Everard was "Mr Hampson's creature" but rather shows that he was keen to use all opportunities to accuse others in order help himself. Everard may have later made use of Robert's hatred of Mary, but in 1671–1673 it does not appear that Everard was in his employment.

However, there is one detail that does indicate Everard may have known Robert; this is Mary's report in her pamphlet that Everard came to her to tell her that Robert's nephew, Thomas Laurence, was in town. This indicates Everard had some knowledge of Robert's family. But this can also be put down to Everard's ability to gather information that might prove useful to him, rather than any actual connection between Hampson and Everard. It may seem odd that Everard concerned himself with such a modest and relatively impoverished person as Mary. However, it must be remembered that Mary was from a well-established and prosperous English family, the Wingfields, and was married to a man of position within the legal community who was the brother of a baronet. Everard may have hoped Mary could be used as some sort of gateway to opportunity, and he was adept at making these connections.

In Paris that early summer of 1671, Everard quickly moved from the modest target of Mary to a much larger opportunity. He appears to have entered into the service of the Duke of Monmouth, Charles II's eldest illegitimate son, or at least to have made some connection in the circle surrounding the duke. The exact capacity in which he served the duke or his circle is unclear. We have only Mary's report of Everard's boast that he was in the duke's service. Unfortunately, Everard's practice of lying is so well documented that nothing he said (or wrote) can be trusted. One small example of his practice of lying even in minor matters can be seen in Everard's tale to Mary concerning a book he carried in his pocket when the two met accidentally at Louis XIV's palace at St. Germaine (now in the suburbs of Paris). Mary wrote that Everard took out this book and showed it to her. He claimed there was only one copy in France and the Duke of Anguien used the very copy he now had to ward off danger. In fact this book, the *Enchiridion Leonis Papae Serenissimo Imperatori*

Carolo Magno, was a popular and widely available French grimoire, or spell book, probably written in the sixteenth century; it was printed in several editions for more than a hundred years. Apparently he wished to sell the book to Mary. For Everard, no opportunity to lie and make even a small profit was missed.

It does seem very unfortunate that Mary continued to cross his path. Whether this was simply bad fortune or something more sinister is unclear. Her personal difficulties and his rather more spectacular ability to get into trouble came together again in late 1673. Mary had returned to England in an attempt to collect her alimony. She recounts in her pamphlet that shortly before her departure Everard appeared at her lodging in Paris begging her to take him with her back to England, even promising to act as her servant. Mary says she refused but, pitying him, gave him a meal. Everard did make it back to England, where he was quickly arrested on charges that he intended to poison the Duke of Monmouth or some other important person. Before his arrest, Mary relates in her pamphlet how Everard came to visit her at the Fiennes' house, where she was staying. She noted he was injured and looked haggard. Shortly after his arrest, Mary was summoned to appear before Henry Coventry, the secretary of state, who was carrying out the investigation concerning Everard and his alleged plot. In her pamphlet, Mary says she thought she was summoned to Coventry because of Louis XIV's letter supporting her attempts to receive her alimony. Instead, she recounts her shock to find that Coventry wanted to speak to her because of Everard's accusation that she planned to murder her husband. In 1679 Everard would put this accusation in print in the pamphlet mentioned above. In this printed version of Everard's tale of Mary's murderous intent, he produced a compelling narrative that drew upon cultural portraits of the murderous wife:

> Mrs. Wingfield, alias Hampton, a Benchers wife of the Temple, then also in Paris, went also about to all English gentlemen there to avenge her quarrels against her husband, who as they say (not without some good cause) has cast her off: She applied her self to me, who not approving of those violent means, I obtained for her a Letter of Recom-

mendation for Justice to be done to her, from the French King to the King of England; signed by Secretary Pompone, directed to Secretary Arlington in England: This was in 73, but she not finding any good by this letter, she went on to propose to me her old ways; So seeing her incorrigible, fearing she would fall into worse hands, and hoping to get back the money I had lent to her and laid out for her; I kept in with her till she could get money to pay me: but finding no hopes of either the one or the other, I bid this Dallison my man, to take her in hand, to pretend to close to her designs, till I could get my money. I directed him to her lodgings, but he told me that Sir Robert Welsh and himself knew her well enough: And that he would get me one Johnson a student in physick, who would act his part in the comedy better than any. I told them I would share with them both of what was due to me by this woman, and what besides they could get from her: She proffered to give some hundreds of pounds, then in the hands of Monsieur de Basti in London, and her daughter besides in marriage, to any that would kill her husband by the sword, poyson, &c. But finding she could not perform the payment of a far less sum due to me, and that to receive into my company persons of so wicked principles in religion and moralities, was scandalous; I cast them all off in Paris.

Here Everard links Mary's murderous intent to insinuations that she was cast off by Robert "with good cause," which would be read by contemporaries as adultery. In seventeenth-century English culture, women's violence was linked to their sexual appetites, which, uncontrolled, were feared to lead to terrible crimes, such as the murder of a disliked or discarded spouse. Everard portrays her desperation through her exaggerated speech and a description of her immodest actions as she goes about to "all English gentlemen" with tales of her woes and pleas for revenge. This activity of "going about" contains the suggestion of illicit sexual activity, as does the comment "that Sir Robert Welsh and himself knew her well enough." He also suggests in this pamphlet that she was a Roman Catholic and thus an even more suspicious and corrupt person. After establishing the wickedness of her character, he describes her murderous plan, using stock representations of the murderous wife found in popular drama, cheap pamphlets and ballads, books of advice and admonishment, and even legal treatises of the time. These representations showed the stock actions of the adulterous and passionate wife, including the assembling of co-conspirators—often men of low character—the payment in gold or marriage, and the use of poison, swords, or daggers. This stock depiction of the murderous wife was also used by Robert in his accusations against Mary in his Court of Arches and High Court of Delegates depositions. As discussed in Chapter One, Robert accused Mary of threatening to poison him with kisses, and of stabbing him with a penknife, though Robert told his tale with less flare and imagination than Everard. In fact, accusations that women attempted to poison or stab husbands were commonly employed to discredit women in a variety of circumstances, and reveal male anxiety concerning what they believed to be the volatile nature of women.[17]

Everard, after establishing Mary's character through these stock motifs, goes on to link her to wider criminal and treasonous activity:

> She some weeks before came over unknown to me into England, but the next day after my arrival here, I met her accidentally, and she brought me to her lodging . . . Also she there in Paris met with the Talbots every night, and with Sir Robert Welsh; amongst them it was contrived that Dallison should come over into England, and turn these petit matters wherein I seemed to comply with these Ladies, as if I intended them against the Duke of Monmouth, for not payment of arrears, &c. and by this means they thought to blast my discovery of the plot against them, when I came into England; and that I would be certainly secured when I arrived there: and they had the assurance to threaten me there-with to my face. Their threats came punctually to pass, for I was secured according to their contrivance within a few days after I was in London.

In this interesting narrative turn, Everard tries to convince his readers that the accusation against him—that he planned to poison the Duke of Monmouth—was actually an elaborate scheme concocted by several people, Mary among them, to stop him from exposing their "petit" or personal crimes. It may be that his verbal testimony to Coventry was less colorful than this later printed version, but it contained enough material to convince the authorities to question Mary.[18]

However, it is likely that Coventry's real interest in meeting with Mary was not the accusations against her but the information she could provide about Edmund Everard and his life in Paris. Given Everard's accusations against her, it is very likely she gave Coventry all the information she had about Everard. Coventry put him in prison on the basis of evidence from Mary and others. Coventry clearly did not believe she intended to murder Robert because he released her after questioning and allowed her to leave the country. This interrogation clearly frightened her, and rather than pursuing Robert further for her alimony, she returned to France shortly afterward in January 1674. This may have contributed to Robert's confidence in asserting publicly and in legal documents that she was dead. Mary's chance encounter with Everard thus cost her more than the price of her gold watch. Unfortunately, her relationship with him was not at an end, as Everard stood poised to inflict greater damage to her reputation and create even more difficulties for her in her attempts to collect alimony and live the quiet life she so desired.

Everard was released from prison in 1678, after convincing the authorities he could provide valuable service as a spy. Yet despite his long imprisonment and his new job as a government spy, he did not forget the unfortunate Mary Hampson. Mary tells of a strange encounter with Everard in early February 1678, shortly after his release from prison, that shows he had not forgotten her. She describes in her pamphlet how he came to her lodging and attempted to speak to her in French. Wisely, she refused to speak to him in that language, preferring English so the other woman present could understand what was said. Mary says Everard left her then, but in 1679 he published his pamphlet, and it was here that he recounted his fabrication of her plot to kill her husband.[19] This story was later read out, as Mary describes it, in her meeting with Robert in 1680 in front of the judges of the High Court of Delegates during one of her attempts to collect alimony. It was this encounter with Robert that turned into the mob attack outside the Inner Temple that she described to Sir William Trumbull. Robert may have felt free to treat Mary in this way because of the damage done to her reputation by Everard's published story of her murder plot.

Mary returned to Europe, this time to the Netherlands in 1680, no doubt hoping never to be troubled with Edmund Everard again, yet who should appear on the scene in November 1682 but Everard. This time he was working as a spy for the English ambassador, Bevill Skelton, using Everard to spy on the English community in the Netherlands, and also to monitor the printing of antigovernment material that might be smuggled for distribution in England.[20] Mary recalls in her pamphlet that Everard lodged at the house of the Rotterdam printer Henry Goddaeus, who lived at number 3 in the Newstreet. What she does not mention in her pamphlet is that she lodged with the Goddaeus family in 1681, sending letters from there to Sir William Trumbull in April, May, and June of that year. It may even be that for a short time she and Everard both lodged with Goddeaus. But it is more likely that Everard's arrival in Rotterdam precipitated her return to Paris, where she is reported living in June 1683.

Goddeaus was also the printer of the first edition of Mary's pamphlet. She accuses Everard, in the London printing of the pamphlet, of burning the first edition in Rotterdam at Robert's request, for, she believed, "it must be by Mr. Hampson's means, for the said Everard had no power, nor was in a condition to subborn the printer." What Mary did not know was that Everard, as an agent for the English government, did have the means to force the printer to burn the pamphlets because of the authority given to him by Ambassador Skelton—though this was intended to stop the printing and distribution of political pamphlets only. It seems most probable that Everard misused this power to order Mary's pamphlets destroyed, perhaps hoping to be rewarded by Robert.

One tantalizing piece of evidence suggests that Robert may not have even realized Mary's pamphlets had been destroyed. In discussing the attempts of Francis Burke to collect her alimony, Mary complains in her pamphlet that Robert told Burke "he would not pay [the alimony] unless he know the place and house where I lived, and that I should call in this Relations [her pamphlet] which I caused to be printed at Rotterdam." Mary calls this a very unnecessary demand and then goes on to explain that Everard had already burnt the pamphlets. This may indicate Everard was not in contact with Robert at all, but he destroyed Mary's pamphlets as some form of personal revenge against her. It may even be that Everard informed Robert about Mary's pamphlet but did not tell him all copies had been burned. In any case, guessing the allegiances and motivations of Edmund Everard was always difficult. Even Ambassador Skelton complained that Everard "juggles with me . . . [and] playes fast & loose of all sides."[21]

It is difficult to know what to make of the many (of what appear to be coincidental) meetings between Mary and Everard. Certainly her association with one of the most notorious informers of the time added tremendously to the difficulties she faced after her separation from Robert. It is also difficult to understand why Everard continued to meddle in her affairs. She believed he was Robert's agent, paid to torment her, but there is no evidence Robert ever employed Everard. In fact it would have been incredibly foolhardy for Robert, in his position as a sergeant of law and respected member of the legal community, to become entangled with Everard given the latter's reputation. Others who became associated with Everard paid a heavy price. Sir Robert Walsh, who was mentioned in association with Mary in Everard's pamphlet, ended up in prison. Edward Fitzharris was executed because of Everard's manipulations and lies. Mary considered her unfortunate association with Everard as one of the many trials set before her to test her spirit.

The years following her separation from Robert were not easy ones for Mary. Her futile attempts to secure her alimony, and her rootless life, which took her back and forth between continental Europe and England, made it difficult for her to live in respectable retirement. For Robert, initially the situation was quite different. Despite the humiliation of his marital problems, he managed to continue his professional advancement. In his personal life he also had some success, especially in arranging an advantageous marriage between his eldest daughter Elizabeth and Charles Bill. Their wedding was held in the Inner Temple church in 1681. Robert had also reconciled with his family. His sister Katherine called him her "dear brother" and left Robert and his daughters money and property in her will in 1678. Finally, if Mary's accusation is to be believed, Robert had even secured himself the comfort of a new wife or mistress. And yet, despite all this apparent success, Robert's inability to turn financial opportunity into long-lasting financial security plagued him, as is shown by the events in 1683.

In 1672, Robert had been given permission to construct two buildings in the Inner Temple consisting of eight chambers, or apartments.[22] They were to replace chambers that had been lost during the Great Fire of 1666. This commission was an opportunity for him to secure a profitable investment, as he would collect rental income on these chambers for "two lives" (approximately thirty years). However, by 1683 the renting out of these chambers became problematic. It appears that Robert, or the men who rented the chambers in "Serjeant Hampson's Buildings" as they were called, had allowed nonmembers of the Inner Temple to live in them, which was against Inner Temple rules. On May 1, 1683, a search was ordered in Robert's buildings, where "several persons lodge with their families, that are not members of this society [the Inner Temple] against the orders of the House." On May 15 the Inner Temple authorities commanded that "the gentlemen concerned in Serjeant Hampson's Buildings do attend the Bench Table touching the lodging of strangers." On May 16 Luke Cropley and John Higden, and "all other strangers" or nonmembers of the Inner Temple, were ordered to leave their lodgings in Hampson's buildings. Cropley petitioned to be admitted to membership in the Inner Temple. This was rejected on June 16, when he received a final order to leave the chamber he occupied in Hampson's buildings.

At this point what appears to have been a dispute over the right to reside in Hampson's buildings turned deadly. These buildings were number 8 and 9 Kings Walk. Sir Thomas Robinson's building was number 7. On the first of August 1683 Robinson's building caught fire. Sir Thomas,

FIGURE 7. Serjeant Hampson's building, no. 9 (built in 1672), King's Bench Walk, Inner Temple, London. Photograph by author.

in an attempt to escape the flames, jumped out of his window to his death. Hampson's staircase number 8, with all four of its chambers, was also destroyed, though no other lives were lost. It was believed at the time that the fire began in an adjoining coffee house, but an investigation into the negligence of the officers and watchmen was ordered. Though there is no evidence at present that the eviction of unauthorized tenants in Hampson's buildings 8 and 9 in July and the fire that followed two weeks later that destroyed buildings 7 and 8 were connected, it is a suggestive coincidence. In any event, Robert saw several hundred pounds of his investment go up with the flames. In October 1683, John Blincoe, John Lee, Walter Burdett, and William Yorke, who had taken chambers in Robert Hampson's building number 8, asked that the Inner Temple authorities set a reasonable value on what was left of the building and force Robert to release his financial interest. These men would later be granted permission to rebuild the chambers, and another of Hampson's hopeful investments ended in disaster.[23]

Mary's pamphlet describing the monstrous behavior of Robert Hampson was published in 1684, with his reply, *A Relation of the Design of Mrs. Hampson to Poison or Stab her Husband*, appearing the following year. The second edition of her pamphlet likely appeared after Robert published his pamphlet. His decision to publish any response at all indicates that he felt Mary's pamphlet did so much damage to his reputation that he had to respond in print, despite the humiliation of drawing further public attention to his marital problems. Their daughter Mary would later recall that Robert told her that her mother was "the occasion of reducing him to a mean condition,"[24] in other words, of reducing him to poverty. This would suggest that in the final years of Robert's life decades of misguided financial investments, and some degree of monetary misfortune, left him in a much reduced financial position, for which he blamed Mary. Robert died in 1688 and was buried in the Inner Temple church among the medieval Knights Templar and later members of the Inner Temple society. His choice of burial place suggests that his relationship to this institution was much stronger than his ties to his family, whose chapel in the old St. Nicholas's Church, Taplow, was the resting place of many Hampsons, including Robert's father and brother.[25]

With Robert's death, Mary's material prospects should have improved dramatically. The income of the property left to her by her uncle, John Whalley, was now hers, and by later accounts it was worth about £100 per year. Mary continued to have some influential friends in England, among them Mary and William Montagu. She no longer had to fear Robert's hatred and could reasonably expect to settle into a modest life in England, perhaps even reconciling with her daughters. Unfortunately, the years of conflict with Robert would continue to trouble her for the rest of her life.

Chapter 3
THE WIDOW HAMPSON *and* HER DAUGHTERS

Even after Robert's death, problems from her marriage continued to plague Mary Hampson. She had difficulties claiming the rental income from the property her uncle John Whalley had left her, which led to more harrowing adventures. Her attempts to claim this income resulted in a bitter lawsuit between her daughters and herself, effectively destroying any chance of a reconciliation between them. Mary finally settled in the home of the widow Mary Opaven, in the parish of St Brides, London, where she lived out her last days with Mary Opaven and Opaven's daughter, another Mary, in what was later reported as a quiet and dignified retirement. On Mary Hampson's death, there was renewed hostility over the property Whalley had left Mary. This led to another flurry of lawsuits, this time between the young Mary Opaven and Mary Hampson's daughters.

Mary Hampson was living, as she describes it, "beyond the seas," in continental Europe when Robert Hampson died in November 1688. Given that his death meant she could claim the rents from the lands in Huntingdonshire left to her by her uncle John Whalley, one might suppose that Mary would have quickly returned to England, or at least made swift arrangements to have the rents from these properties sent over to her in continental Europe. Yet this did not happen. For more than a year after his death, Mary lived in ignorance of the event. In a suit she took out against her daughters, she explains that she learned Robert Hampson was dead in "or about" 1690, and that she returned to England in February 1692 to collect these rents.[1] The fact that it took over a year for Mary to hear of Robert's death suggests that after he published his pamphlet accusing her of trying to murder him in 1685, Mary gave up any thoughts of collecting alimony and settled into her life on the continent with the intention of making the best of her situation there. She may have returned to Delft and lodged with the Van Opaven family, where she had once stayed in 1680. Later, Mary would live with a Mrs. Opaven in London and in her will would leave that woman's daughter, Mary Opaven, all her personal property and her land in Huntingdonshire. In Mary's will she says she does this because of "her [the young Mary's] kindness and long assistance to me and in consideration of obligations I have to her father and relations."[2]

By February 1692, Mary's circumstances appear to have changed, and she returned to England to claim the income from her property. Unfortunately, on her return she found that her daughters and her son-in-law, Charles Bill, were determined to keep this income, which they had claimed since Robert's death. Mary's children went so far as to claim their mother had died. By the time Mary returned to England, her daughter Elizabeth had been married to Charles for eleven years. He was the head of a household that included not only Elizabeth but also her sister Mary. The many legal suits Bill was engaged in through the years would often list this Mary along with Elizabeth as witnesses, suggesting that Mary Hampson's younger daughter remained unmarried and made her home with the Bills at least through 1707.

This marriage, which would later cause Mary so many problems, took place in 1681. Charles was the grandson of John Bill, one of the king's printers, who made his fortune through the printing of the Authorized, or King James, Version of the Bible. Charles's mother was Lady Diana Bill, second daughter of Mildmay Fane, Earl of Westmorland. Charles inherited the 460 acre estate of Kenwood on his father's death (which he later sold). Through the marriage of Elizabeth Hampson and Charles Bill, Robert Hampson no doubt hoped to see his grandchildren move from their gentry roots in the Hampson and Wingfield families to enter the aristocracy through Charles's connections with the Earls of

Westmorland, though in the end the marriage does not appear to have produced any surviving children.

Unfortunately for Mary Hampson, Charles appears to have gained a taste for legal actions and was unrelenting in his pursuit of Mary's small property holding. Mary claims in her suit that Charles and Elizabeth Bill sent people to her lodging to harass her, and they told her neighbors she was a cheat and an imposter. Mary told the court:

> Charles Bill and Mary Hampson did make the said tenant [William Baker] believe [she] was not the widow of Serjeant Hampson but was a counterfeit and sent several persons to [her] lodgings to give out that [she] was a cheat as aforesaid in so much that [she] was forced for her safety to apply herself to William Montagu esquire, late Lord Chief Baron of the Exchequer.[3]

Charles, and Mary Hampson's two daughters, Elizabeth and Mary, denied that they ever called Mary Hampson a "counterfeit" or "cheat." However, their testimony in many ways confirms that they at least suggested they did not believe Mary was their mother.

Bill states that Mary had been "for many years beyond the seas" and that he heard she was dead.[4] He and Elizabeth further stated that they would be willing to give an account of the rents received from the Huntingdonshire property "*if* [my emphasis] the said Mary Hampson be living, neither of these defendants [Charles and Elizabeth] well knowing the person of the said Mary Hampson having not seen her for many years." Charles went on to claim that the only evidence he had received proving that Mary Hampson was indeed his wife's mother was the word of William Montagu. One would think that the word of a former Baron of the Exchequer and a completely disinterested party would in most circumstances be enough to convince anyone of Mary's identity, especially as Charles and Elizabeth admitted they had not seen her for many years. Yet the couple refused to relinquish the rents they had received from Mary's property. By the time Charles and Elizabeth made this statement, they had been denying Mary's identity for two years, despite Montagu's identification of Mary Hampson, as niece of John Whalley, widow of Robert Hampson, and mother of Elizabeth Bill and Mary Hampson. In fact, Mary even submitted the letter Montagu wrote for her to the court, which is also quoted in her deposition. The letter states:

These [words] are to certify whom it may concern that this gentlewoman the bearer hereof is the widow of Mr. Serjeant Hampson and was the daughter of Bodenham Wingfield esquire and the niece of Mr. John Whalley. I have known her a long time and therefore assert it under my hand, William Montagu, 17th March 1692.

On receiving this letter, which they could easily have verified by contacting Montagu directly, the Bills and the daughter Mary Hampson should have relinquished their rights to the rental income of Mary's property and refunded her the rents they had collected since 1688. It appears they had no intention of parting with any money and so continued to deny that Mary Hampson was alive. In addition, they inserted another argument into their defense, one that had no legal basis but that they hoped might influence the court into looking more favorably on their actions.

Elizabeth Bill states that she was "removed from her [Mary's] presence" at a very young age and bred up with her aunt Katherine Hampson, who had a "love and affection for" her. Again the inference here is that she was removed from her mother's care because Mary was not a fit mother. Mary's other daughter, Mary, is even more explicit in her deposition, stating that her mother "having for several years before the said Mr. Serjeant Hampson died eloped from him and been the occasion of reducing him to a mean condition as this defendant hath heard."[5] She also states, though Charles and Elizabeth Bill do not, that "great inquiry by the [London] Gazette otherwise had been made" for the whereabouts of Mary Hampson. However, there is no advertisement or inquiry in the archived issues of the London Gazette requesting information on Mary Hampson between 1688 and 1691.[6]

The daughter, Mary, also attempted to engage the sympathy of the court by presenting herself as impoverished. She complains to the court in her testimony that she was left "in mean circumstances" and that she never had more than nineteen pounds in total from the rents paid. The young Mary may not have been overstating her financial situation here. Robert must have provided a generous financial settlement for Elizabeth Hampson in order to make her a reasonable marital prospect for the young Charles Bill, grandson of an earl. In addition, Elizabeth inherited the bulk of her aunt Katherine Hampson's estate, which amounted to approximately £1,500. Her sister Mary was left money and goods worth about £400. Apparently there was no money left to entice an eligible suitor for Mary. Instead, she lived with her sister until at least as late as 1707, when we lose sight of her. Mary thus attempted to court the sympathy of the judge in order to lessen any blame that might fall on her.

However, Mary Hampson's accusation that the Bills and her daughter Mary were in a "confederacy" or in league with the tenants of the Huntingdonshire property, Baker and Pickard, is probably incorrect. Instead, the situation was much more complicated, with each party attempting to protect its own interests, which sometimes intersected and sometimes diverged. William Baker states in his deposition that he first leased Close Pasture, Lord Pasture, Head Close, and Ashton Close in the parish of Wistow, Huntingdonshire (Mary's property), in about 1674 from Robert Hampson. He then explains that John Blimston, Robert's bailiff (or receiver of his rents) in Huntingdonshire, was the first to tell him of Robert and Mary's deaths.

John Blimston was in contact with the Bills and the daughter Mary, and he continued to do business with them, purchasing in 1694 the 219 acres in Raveley Fen the women had inherited from their father.[7] If, as Baker stated, Blimston had told him of Mary Hampson's death, he was acting on the instructions of the Bills and the young Mary. Baker continues in his testimony to portray his involvement in the situation as that of a conscientious businessman. He says that he went to London in May 1689 and met with Charles Bill, who suggested Baker keep the rent that should have been paid to the daughter Mary. It is unclear why Bill would suggest this, and Baker says nothing about the much larger portion that he paid to Bill for Elizabeth's part of the land. Baker also says he was forced to pay some of the daughter Mary's money, because she threatened to have him arrested for nonpayment. Here it appears Baker and Bill were attempting to shift attention and blame onto the daughter Mary, though this seems a particularly weak strategy and it is unclear what they hoped to accomplish. The daughter, Mary Hampson, in her testimony gives a more detailed account of Baker's dealings. She says that Charles Bill gave both Baker and Pickard bonds "or writing" that would secure them against any demand for money should her mother actually be alive. She also states she did not know how much money Baker and Pickard agreed to give Bill. Apparently she also did not know that Bill offered to allow Baker to keep her portion of the rents. The daughter Mary's testimony was certainly designed to place Bill as legally liable for the rents that were paid, though it also confirms that Bill and Baker did consult and come to some sort of arrangement.

In his deposition, Baker says he became aware that Mary Hampson was alive sometime in 1692, and that he immediately wrote to her concerning the property he was leasing. Mary brought this letter to court, and it is entered in her suit. In the letter, Baker agrees to meet with Mary concerning the rents, and he claims he was led astray by the Bills and the daughter, Mary:

> Madam this is to let you understand that I have all the lands in use in Bury [leased from] Serjeant Hampson except a small piece of about three pounds a year and am sorry your daughters knowing as you relate it that you was alive satisfied the contrary to me threatening to sue me and did sue the other tenant [Pickard]. However when I heard per chance last year that you was alive I refused to pay them anymore rent. There are sums of money belonging to the rent which they differed about that still remaineth in my hands which I intend to wait upon you with in London the first week in April next to pass my accounts and pay you your money. This from Madam your servant William Baker, March 20th 1692.[8]

Mary decided not to wait for Baker to come to London but instead traveled to Huntingdonshire. However, she explains in her suit that Baker refused to pay her because she would not sign the document he had prepared. Mary believed this document to be some type of ruse or "design," intended to defraud her. She believed that by signing the document she would be releasing her interest in the rents Baker had paid to the Bills and her daughter Mary. Legally, all Mary was required to do was provide Baker with a note acknowledging her receipt of whatever money he paid her. She also relates in her suit that Charles Bill had earlier told Baker not to give Mary anything because she was poor and could not launch any sort of legal challenge. Baker, no doubt finding himself in a position where he could avoid paying the rents to anyone for a time, took Bill's advice.

Mary Hampson certainly presented herself to the court as a very impoverished widow. At one point in her testimony, she describes how she was forced to walk from "London to Bury in Huntingdonshire being about fifty miles distant."[9] This at first appears to be the sort of exaggeration one often sees in court documents. However, Baker's statement corroborates Mary's condition. He remarks that "hearing of her necessities and on seeing her then circumstances" he was "moved to compassion" for her,[10] though that compassion obviously did not extend to actually paying Mary the money he owed her. Baker's statement also reveals that there were at least three people who were willing to assist Mary in her destitute condition when she arrived in Huntingdonshire: Mistress James, Owen Fann, and Madam Headley. In the heraldic visitation of Huntingdonshire in 1684,[11] Owen Fann is listed as a member of the gentry in the town of Ramsey, as is Mistress James and Madam Headley. Madam Headley is also recorded as having a son who was an officer in the Guards in London. Interestingly, William Baker is listed on this visitation as "disclaimed"; that is, he had no right to style himself as a gentleman.[12]

The legal documents relating to this case are incomplete, but Mary Hampson's later will and attempts by her daughters and Charles Bill to challenge it reveal that Mary Hampson was successful in claiming the small inheritance left to her by her uncle, John Whalley. The evidence emerging from the challenge to her will shows that, in the final years of her life, Mary lived quietly as a respectable widow in the household of Mrs. Mary Opaven, and Opaven's daughter Mary. These three Marys lived together for six years, and it is clear that Mary Hampson became very fond of the young Mary. In her will Mary says she bequeaths her goods to this young Mary for her "kindness and long assistance to me."[13] She also mentions the "obligations" she had to Mary Opaven's father and relations for all the help they provided her in the past. In her letters to William Trumbull in the 1680s, Mary mentions Mr. George Van Opaven in Delft, who received her letters and helped manage her affairs at that time. It is likely that this George was the young Mary Opaven's father or a close relative. Mary's gratitude led her to leave the Huntingdonshire property to the young Mary Opaven, and it was this bequest that resulted in Charles Bill and the Hampson sisters' challenging their mother's will.

After Mary Hampson's death, the Bills and the daughter Mary were quick to launch a challenge against her will, and certainly there were some irregularities relating to it; the most glaring was that Mary Hampson had not actually signed it. Mary Opaven's guardian was a gentleman named Robert Arundel; he defended the will on behalf of the young Mary. His statement reveals a deep animosity between Mary Hampson and her daughters. He recalls that:

> The aforesaid Elizabeth Bill and Mary Hampson her daughters gave out and declared that she was likewise dead and died in a ditch and thereupon received her rents of her lands during such her absence and converted the same to their own use, so that she [Mary Hampson] was forced to return home for want of maintenance abroad and being returned they the said Elizabeth Bill and Mary Hampson refused to pay her what they had received of her rents during her said absence so that she was put into great straights, and had starved had she not been relieved by Mrs. Opaven alias Uphoven mother of the aforesaid Mary Opaven.

The stinging phrase "died in a ditch" has a sense of orality and theatricality about it that one could imagine Mary Hampson using as she bitterly recalled her struggles with her daughters on her return to England in 1692. Arundel also asserts in his statement that there was no reconciliation between the mother and daughters, claiming

> That the said Elizabeth Bill and Mary Hampson continued in their
> undutifulness to their mother . . . to the time of her death and that the
> said Mary did thereupon several times as well in her health as in her last
> sickness whereof she died seriously declare that she would give nothing
> to them when she died or used words to the same effect.[14]

Given the statements made by both Elizabeth Bill and the daughter Mary Hampson in the court documents of 1693–94, this portrayal of the state of the relationship between Mary and her daughters in the final years of Mary Hampson's life is probably fairly accurate. However, the last-minute writing of the will and Arundel's explanation as to why the will was not signed seems constructed.

Arundel states in court records that on February 14, 1698, Mary Hampson, entering into her last sickness, decided to write her will. Certainly Mary could have written an earlier will and may have decided to change this one in order to leave her property to Mary Opaven. This in itself is not an unreasonable explanation concerning why she waited until she was only hours from death to write her will. In any case, Arundel explains that she did make her will the day of her death by orally instructing a scribe of her final wishes. Again, there is nothing out of the ordinary in this. However, before she actually signed the will, Arundel reports that Mary had a "fit of the gripes" or spasms in the bowel and was not able to sit up and sign it. The witnesses who had assembled to watch Mary sign the will left at that time, agreeing to return later when she was feeling better. That evening, Arundel states that Mary's illness "being much abated [she] did about five or six of the clock of the evening of the aforesaid day rise out of her bed and sat by the fireside"[15] and waited for the witnesses to return. However, only one witness arrived, and Mary was forced to send for the other. It is unclear who was in the room at this time, though from the way in which Arundel phrases his statement it sounds as though he was in the room. This would suggest he was the only adult with Mary at that time. This would mean the will could not be validated because doing so required two adult witnesses. While Mary Hampson, Robert Arundel, and perhaps the young Mary Opaven waited for the second witness, Arundel states that Mary said "she did approve of her aforesaid will and of what she had given to the aforesaid Mary Opaven alias Uphoven and that the same should stand for and be her last will and testament."[16] This may indeed have been what Mary said as they waited, though it is more likely that either her statement of intent was reshaped in the reporting of it in order to function as binding a legal statement, or she may have chosen to frame her wishes in this manner so that Arundel could later swear to this statement. Both Mary and Arundel would understand that this statement created a nuncupative or voiced will. Unfortunately, without a second adult witness this type of voiced will would have some difficulty being proved. Still, even without a second witness, Arundel hoped to shore up his larger narrative of Mary's dying intentions by reporting her voiced intentions, which could then sit alongside the unsigned will.

Whatever the actual truth about the last day of Mary's life, Arundel did convince the court that the unsigned will was Mary Hampson's legitimate last will and testament. Sir Richard Raines, Doctor of Laws of the Prerogative Court of Canterbury, found in Mary Opaven's favor and ordered that she was to receive the inheritance left to her by Mary Hampson "just as is contained in the aforesaid will according to the intention and by the force of the aforesaid will."[17] Unsurprisingly, Arundel had difficulties collecting Mary Opaven's rental income from William Baker and John Pickard. In the end Arundel sued Baker and Pickard, and his statement provides additional insight into the character of these two men.[18]

In this suit, Arundel asks for one year of rental arrears of £100 due on Mary Hampson's Huntingdonshire property that Baker rented. Arundel explains in the suit that Mary had died and her will was proved or found valid by the courts, and thus the property now belonged to Mary Opaven. He also explains that John Newman, the executor of Mary's will, had taken out letters of administration and was authorized to execute the will—that is, to collect the rents for Mary Opaven. Arundel states that William Baker and John Pickard said they did not owe the arrears. Arundel also claims, most outrageously, that they claimed they never knew Mary Hampson, which confirms that Baker was continuing his slippery business practices, as the many documents connected with Mary Hampson's legal action in 1693 to 1694 proves that Baker was well acquainted with Mary. From Arundel's suit, we also learn that Mary received the rental income from her property during the last years of her life and that the income was £100 per year. No verdict regarding this suit survives, and it is likely that in the end Baker and Pickard, after trying their luck yet again, resumed their rental payments.

Through these legal documents we are given one final glimpse into Mary Hampson's life, so often filled with conflict, poverty, and at times real danger. Her estrangement from her daughters and the loss of her social position reveal the inability of social institutions to protect women in troubled marriages. The actions of Robert Hampson, Charles Bill, Edmund Everard, and even William Baker illustrate how men could use legal and state institutions to protect their own interests at the expense of the vulnerable, especially women. There is little to respect or admire in the stories of any of these men, at least in their behavior toward Mary Hampson. And yet, her story is also filled with men and women who go to some lengths to help her. Granted, their exertions were not always successful, and one sometimes suspects that Mary's pleas for help were at times unwanted and a nuisance. It is also difficult to understand how the many powerful allies Mary had could allow her to suffer so much and sink so low, though this is not unusual in stories about women in Mary's situation. Yet the fact remains that without the exertions of these men and women—the Montagus, the Opavens, the Fiennes, the merchants and bankers who carried her messages, the French nobility that gave her lodging and friendship, Robert Arundel and John Newman, and the many other friends and strangers who offered her assistance during her life—Mary would not have survived into what were her final, peaceful, years of life.

Mary's "Last Will and Testament" was more than simply a formal document through which she fulfilled her final cultural obligation. Instead, it was a triumphant statement of Mary's own intentions and an affirmation of her personhood and identity. In this will, Mary Hampson repudiated her marriage in the strongest terms, choosing an adopted daughter, Mary Opaven, to replace the two living daughters she had with Robert. She also imposed her own "will" on her uncle, one of the major instigators of her marriage. According to the portion of his will quoted in legal documents in 1664, John Whalley left his property in Wistow and Bury, Huntingdonshire, to Mary Hampson and the "heirs of her body."[19] In 1698 Mary chose instead to leave this small estate to the heir of her affection, the young Mary Opaven. Through her will, Mary was able to provide the young and orphaned Mary with the financial means to live her own life, rather than suffer in the way Mary Hampson had suffered, through the well-intentioned, but ultimately disastrous, efforts of others.

CONCLUSIONS

In a letter to William Trumbull, Mary Hampson claimed that because Robert Hampson had taken a new wife she was "free before God" and hoped that she "would be free before the world as I am before God."[1] In her pamphlet she insists that:

> All these and many other false and cruel actions which Mr. Hampson hath practised to oppress my innocence, and make me miserable in this world, does and hath assured me, and will in Gods good time, make appear unto all good and intelligent persons, that Mr. Hampson's leaving of me was a cruel, scandalous, and malicious desertion, which by the laws of all countrys sets the innocent party free.

In both her statement to Trumbull and this passage in her pamphlet, Mary was not simply indulging in the desperate wishes of an oppressed woman. Rather, she shows that she was aware of the controversies surrounding marriage that emerged in the sixteenth and seventeenth centuries. In these controversies existed tensions among customary practice, religious authority, and emerging ideas from Protestant reformists[2] that considered the nature of the matrimonial bond.

One of the most eloquent spokespersons for the ideal nature of marriage within the Protestant reformist tradition was the poet John Milton. He was perhaps encouraged to consider these ideals and the institution of marriage itself when he experienced the almost immediate collapse of his marriage to Mary Powell in 1642. In the four pamphlets that followed,[3] Milton presents an ideal portrait of marriage where a couple "love one another to the height of dearness," fulfilling the roles of their gender with a generous spirit. The husband would "bear himself as the head and preserver of his wife, instructing her to all Godlines[s] and integrity of life" and the "wife also be to her husband a help, according to her place." He also stated that within this union the couple would generously share in a "conjugal benevolence" that included sexual intimacy. Milton believed that a marriage so constituted would further both religious devotion and civil concord.[4] In this, Milton was not proposing anything particularly new. In fact, he draws on the work of the sixteenth-century Protestant reformer Martin Bucer in describing his ideal marriage, and he would later use this model in constructing the relationship between his pre-lapsarian Adam and Eve in *Paradise Lost*.

Instead, what modern readers often find surprising is Milton's insistence that when couples find themselves in a disastrous and destructive marriage, they should be allowed to separate and seek a more harmonious marriage with a new partner. He emphasized in his essays the importance of marriage for the spiritual well-being of individuals and the stability of society. This for Milton logically meant that a failed marriage should be ended. Certainly, the Hampson marriage provides excellent support for Milton's claim that contentious marriages were harmful to civil peace given that the Hampsons' marital conflict caused one dangerous street brawl and a number of smaller disturbances. Milton accused those who would not consider the idea of divorce, with the right to remarriage, of hypocrisy, claiming that although they would not allow a couple to remarry after separating (legally or otherwise) "any dishonest associating they permit."[5] In other words, they ignored the fact that by barring a separated couple from remarrying and finding marital harmony, men (and sometimes women) would enter into sexual liaisons. This is what Mary Hampson accuses Robert of doing—of taking a mistress or wife contrary to religious teachings.

Milton also states that society should view marriage through the lens of charity, lamenting "this great and sad oppression which through the strictness of a literal interpreting [of Biblical sources] hath invaded and disturbed the dearest and most peaceable estate of household society."[6] And even though he agrees with his detractors that couples should work to overcome the "infirmities" that often come in marriage, he felt they should not be forced to endure the "outrages" and "perpetual defraudments of truest conjugal society" nor "injuries and vexations as importunate as fire." He agrees that "to endure very much, might doe well as exhortation, but not a compulsive law."[7] In other words, patient endurance of a wayward spouse might be useful advice, spiritually and at times practically, but it should not be forced by law.

It was this compulsion by law that had long concerned many Protestant reformers. Much of Milton's discussion focused on the importance of a companionate and harmonious marriage to enable couples to better fulfil their duties toward God and the commonwealth. However, many Protestant reformers, though interested in this aspect of marriage, were also concerned about authority and jurisdiction. John Hooper, a Protestant minister and later martyr, argued in 1550 that marriage came under the jurisdiction of the civil authorities and not the religious, insisting that marriage was a civil contract rather than a religious sacrament. During Queen Elizabeth's reign, a number of Protestant reformers including Robert Brown, Thomas Cartwright, and William Whately argued for the civil nature of the matrimonial bond as a contract. This view supported the possibility of remarriage for separated couples. Theoretically, if marriage was a civil contract, it was valid only if both parties fulfilled their obligations according to the contract. These arguments are a far cry from present day no-fault divorce, but they suggest a willingness among many to acknowledge the damage to civil society created by spouses locked in conflict, of which the Hampson marriage was certainly an excellent example.[8]

Much of this sixteenth-century debate was concerned with jurisdictional matters and attempts to reconstruct a view and practice of marriage that emphasized Protestant values and conceptions of marriage as companionate and human, as opposed to Roman Catholic insistence on the sacramental and spiritual nature of marriage. Marriage was thus part of a larger debate covering of a range of religious differences between Catholics and Protestants. During the later part of the sixteenth century and until the civil wars of the seventeenth century, these debates waned as Protestant reformers lost influence. However, in 1640, with the relaxation of censorship laws caused by civil unrest, the debate over marriage and calls for divorce that permitted remarriage were renewed, with Milton entering quickly into the public discussion. This discussion was not simply the whimsical imaginings of "what could be." The 1653 "Act touching Marriages and the Registering thereof; and also touching Births and Burials" removed the performance of marriages from the church authorities. Rather than a marriage being solemnized through a religious ceremony, it was now agreed, or contracted. The act also provided greater oversight of marriage. It required that couples prove parental consent. It also required that they convince or prove to the official that they were entering the marriage of their own free will. This act placed the jurisdiction over marriage in the hands of the civil authorities, and until it was revoked after the Restoration of 1660 the civil authorities rather than the church dealt with matters pertaining to marriage.[9]

This desacralizing of marriage opened the way for at least the possibility of divorce when one or both parties violated the contract. Mary Hampson's marriage in 1656 was performed as a civil contract under the stipulations of the 1653 Act. This may be why she often spoke of her marriage as a set of obligations on both sides, and she believed because Robert did not fulfil his commitments made at their marriage, including providing her with a valid jointure free of mortgaged land, their marriage was invalid and she was free before God and the world. Mary may also have been aware that divorce on the basis of its contractual nature was beginning to be allowed in English colonies in America, especially in Massachusetts and Connecticut.[10] Mary's frustrations with the legal practices in England that denied her a complete financial and physical separation from Robert must be seen not only in the personal context of her suffering but within a wider cultural debate where many recognized the desirability, and even necessity in some cases, of the complete severing of a matrimonial bond. Mary's experiences in France would also have convinced her of the failings of the English legal system. In France, married women could sue for control of their own property and the income from it, even within a marriage. Women could also sue for separation of person and property from their husbands, which allowed a woman to live separately on the proceeds of her own estate.[11] This was what Mary was suggesting to William Trumbull when she asked him in 1681 "if there be any way in law . . . to oblige him [Robert Hampson] to returne me part of my estate back."[12]

However, in February 1670, when Mary found herself on the street in New Southampton Square, now Bloomsbury Square, with armed men inside her house refusing her entry, debates concerning the nature of marriage during that time were probably of little interest to her. What she needed on this day was immediate aid, and she found it with her neighbors. Mary likely returned to the Fiennes' house and considered her options. Her concern on this day was not Milton's description of an ideal marriage, but the basic need for money for her support. Milton, and other male writers on marriage in the period, did not unduly concern themselves with the cruel inequities at the heart of the practice of coverture, while Mary was forced to confront them in the most terrifying fashion. In fact these supporters of divorce and remarriage seldom considered the financial question as it related to women in their often eloquent discussions of marriage.

Those like Milton who wrote about the ideal marriage of harmony and mutual support were decidedly quiet on the financial basis of most marriages of the time. The mechanism of this financial basis was the marriage settlement, the financial agreement that preceded most marriages between couples of even very modest financial worth. These financial agreements reveal the deep dissatisfaction and distrust of the arguments used to justify the strictures of coverture where a wife lost all rights to and control of any property. Ideally, coverture was supposed to allow a husband to use all the financial resources available to him in order to better provide for his wife and children both in life and after his death. In reality, there was nothing to compel him to do so, and the number of legal cases accusing husbands or fathers of neglecting their duties in this regard show just how far from the ideal this reality was. Further evidence of social dissatisfaction with the practice of coverture was the widespread use of financial agreements, including jointure agreements and trusts, preceding marriage in England. And yet the marriage agreement itself could introduce tension into a household by placing a portion of the family's property out of the hands of the husband, because, though legally he could sell any marital property, in reality most buyers insisted on the agreement of the wife, to avoid future legal actions on her behalf. In the Hampson household, as in so many others of the period, the tension created by this situation erupted into marital conflict. In her pamphlet, Mary mentions her jointure twenty-one times. Robert revealed his initial dishonesty by including mortgaged land in Mary's jointure agreement. Mary and her uncle, John Whalley, were so worried about her having a suitable jointure because if Robert had died with this original jointure with its mortgaged lands, Mary would have found it difficult to provide for herself and their children. This is also why she continued to insistently return to the subject of her jointure, and why she refused to release any lands connected with her jointure. She also came to see Robert's initial dishonesty as proof of his moral depravity. In the culture, the marriage settlement was not simply a piece of dry legal business that accompanied a marriage. It was part of the agreement that brought the marriage into being. The discovery that Robert had misled Mary and her family in the original marriage agreement undermined the essential trust necessary for a successful marriage.

This financial aspect of marriage continues to resonate today. A 2001 study suggests that "Money is integral to the marital relationship. As such, conflict over its acquisition, accumulation, distribution, and expenditure are commonplace, if not universal."[13] A study in 2009 found that financial conflicts in marriage were "more pervasive, problematic, and recurrent, and remained unresolved, despite including more attempts at problem solving." The study also identifies how the issues concerning money are strongly related to feelings of self-worth and personal vulnerability, and it found that conflicts over money resulted in depression, anger, and defensiveness in partners that, at times, can escalate into marital violence.[14] Mary Hampson would not be surprised by these observations. Nor, indeed, would many of the women whose marital conflicts we find discussed in legal documents from the seventeenth century.

Financial conflict was prevalent in seventeenth-century cases concerning marital conflict. In an examination of court records, the importance of financial matters in the instigation and disintegration of marriages is clear.[15] In these seventeenth-century cases, as in the modern marriages discussed in the studies mentioned above, economic considerations went beyond the simple provision of essential needs. Instead, financial concerns were connected to social status and economic class and were found at every level of the socioeconomic spectrum. Both modern studies and work on seventeenth-century marriage discuss the highly emotive nature of conflicts related to money. These studies reveal that conflicts over money are often about much more than financial security; rather, they serve as an indicator of emotional commitment. This can be seen in Mary's description of her illness (likely depression) after the birth of her fourth child. After explaining that her mother "supplyed my wants in all things," paying for her lodging, food, and medical attention, Mary laments that "the indisposition of my body joyned to the grief I suffered to finde by all Mr. Hampson's actions that he had not any kindness for me, brought me to a very languishing and weak condition." In court depositions, her letters to William Trumbull, and her autobiographical pamphlet, Mary consistently equates Robert's financial neglect with his emotional neglect. As in many modern divorces, Mary believed that her financial contribution to the well-being of the household, as well as her other contributions, entitled her to a reasonable financial settlement when the marriage ended. And, like spouses in many modern marriages, she believed her emotional and physical suffering should become part of the financial calculation—money becoming a surrogate or compensation for the loss of marital contentment.

Of course, unlike modern marriages, Mary's social and financial opportunities after marriage were extremely limited. As discussed previously, even the award of alimony and the right to live separately were little compensation for the high social and financial cost Mary paid for her separation from Robert. In spite of this, she sought separation rather than reconciliation. In this again, there is a long-standing connection between Mary Hampson's choices and those of other women from her own time to the present day. In a study from 2000 looking at divorce filings in America from 1867 to 1995, it was found that 60–70 percent of all divorces were filed by women consistently throughout this period.[16] Since divorce frequently finds women exposed to negative factors such as isolation, loss of financial resources, and social ostracism—especially in earlier centuries—one would logically think that women would avoid divorce or separation if possible; yet this has not been the case. Even in England, from 1570 to 1640, women sued for separation at a slightly higher rate than men, despite, as Mary's story reveals, the incredibly high financial and social cost they paid.[17]

On the face of it, modern studies would appear to be ill suited for providing insight into why women from the sixteenth through the nineteenth centuries chose to end their marriages at a higher rate than men, despite the hardships these women were often forced to endure. However, it is useful to remember that although women today do not generally face the extent of hardship that women endured in the past, divorced and single women continued to suffer economic and social discrimination well into the twentieth century, and many would argue they continue to do so today. Given this, one would expect that until quite recently women would choose to remain in all but the most brutal of marriages. And certainly, in the sixteenth and seventeenth century women generally sought an end to their marriage as a last resort—yet they still chose to end their marriages at a higher rate than men. Mary Hampson's story might go some way in explaining this fact.

Mary told William Trumbull that she lived "in a strange country" because she desired "to live where I am judged by my life and conversation."

In other words, Mary wished to exert the three components of self-determination: "autonomy (feeling uncoerced in one's actions), competence (feeling capable), and relatedness (feeling connected to others)." These, studies suggest, are necessary for a person to have a sense of well-being.[18] The final brutal act of the Hampson marriage, when Mary was locked out of the New Southampton Square house, found her bereft of all of these components. She was ostracized not only from her home but also from her place within her social sphere, and even her ancestry. Through Robert's brutal act Mary became, for a time, a nonperson. Through her court actions, Mary attempted to reassert her sense of self, to reappropriate the right to determine who she was within her community, or as she succinctly put it, "to live where I am judged by my life and conversation." In a society heavily dominated by male privilege, where male rights were insisted on to the detriment of women's rights and indeed well-being, where all institutions of the day insisted on the sublimation of female self-determination in order to ensure male dominance, most women were forced to seek their personal well-being while enduring a very hostile climate. Vestiges of this climate continue to exist in modern Western culture, and perhaps this goes some way to explain why women continue to file for divorce at a higher rate then men, just as they did in previous centuries. Recent research into divorce suggests that women often report feelings of relief, confident they made the correct choice in seeking an end to their marriage. Beyond this qualitative evidence, current studies also present compelling quantitative evidence that women's petitions for divorce, despite the social and financial costs, are a rational response "based on spouses' relative power in the marriage."[19] This returns us to studies that suggest that need fulfillment and self-realization are necessary for a sense of well-being. For many modern women, as for Mary Hampson, self-determination and autonomy is of greater value than any social and financial benefit they may receive in an oppressive marriage.

In many ways, Mary's story fits neatly into the pattern of seventeenth-century (and indeed, later) marital conflicts. Conflict over money matters exacerbated weaknesses in the marital relationship. Robert Hampson's inability to successfully manage material success led to anger and violence. The many attempts of friends, relatives, professionals, and the wider communities in which they lived failed to bring about anything more than temporary reconciliations. Finally, after extracting all Mary had to offer in the marriage of a financial, emotional, and physical nature, Robert threw her out of the house, confident he could defend himself to his legal colleagues if called on to do so. Mary brought her case to the ecclesiastical courts, and the result was a negotiated settlement that would allow each to live separately, with Robert ordered to pay Mary £100 a year in maintenance. Thus far, Mary's story differs little from those of other women who found themselves in similar situations for hundreds of years. However, what makes Mary's story unique is the determined and creative way she went about rebuilding her life as a separate and self-determined individual. She insists several times in the documents associated with her case that she refused to be a "slave"—that is, she would not be owned and demeaned by another human being—rebelling against the legal restrictions of coverture and social expectations that expected she would simply endure betrayal and violence. Robert once accused Mary of announcing that she had a "Roman Spirit." And though he meant she was dangerous and intractable, Mary agreed she had made such a claim, explaining that "she hath sometime said that she had so far a Roman Spirit that she would rather suffer and die than . . . live to be made a slave."[20] Mary may have had in her mind John Paulet's description of just such a Roman Spirit in his *Gallery of Heroick Women* (1652): "the voice of her blood, which is courageous and bold, which is animated with indignation and justice, which is full of a Roman spirit and virtue."[21]

Instead of succumbing to the privations of life, Mary sought again and again to establish herself as an individual, setting up a new life in Paris and the Netherlands, even renaming herself Mary Wingfield in order to escape the calumny of being Mr. Hampson's wife. She fought for eighteen years to force Robert to pay her alimony in spite of his refusals and brutality. She wrote her compelling story and bravely put it to press, not once but three times. She took on her own daughters in order to claim the inheritance that allowed her to live with some degree of dignity in England during her last years. Finally, at her death, it was her "will" that prevailed as she defied her uncle, her daughters, and social expectations to leave her inheritance to a young woman, Mary Opaven. This was perhaps a small victory, but at her death Mary could confidently claim she had lived her life courageously, boldly, and energetically, seeking justice in order to live a life where she determined how she was judged and perceived, rather than existing as the construct of another.

LETTERS *from* MARY HAMPSON
to WILLIAM TRUMBULL (1680–1681)

August 1, 1680:
Doctor Trumbull at his lodgings in Doctor's Commons or at his house near to it.

Sir

The compassion you was pleased to show me in my business gives me the confidence to beg the favor of you to let me know if Mr. Hampson hath paid the fifty pounds the last day of July as was ordered to Mr. Franklin and likewise what way I must take to oblige Mr. Hampson to pay me my alimony I living in a strange country, for if it be possible I would not live in England where my husband by his false reports hath so stained my reputation that I think it not safe for me to live there, for what ever affront is put upon me I find no justice therefore I desire to live where I am judged by my life and conversation and not by the report of a second Mahomet whom would do as the first did, destroy me, so that I may not discover by what unjust ways he is come to credit. The last June having escaped Mr. Hampson's hands I had liked to have been killed by the rabble under the notion that I was a mad woman.[1] These things considered makes me endeavour to live where justice is for me as for others. To this end I write to you sir and desire your counsel and an answer hop-

Letters from Mary Hampson to William Trumbull, D/ED/053, Berkshire Records Office, Reading, UK. These letters are in Mary Hampson's hand. The spelling is very idiosyncratic and so has been updated to modern usage. William Trumbull was a lawyer, diplomat, and government official. He was knighted in 1684.

ing you will do for me what may be done and that you will believe me to be grateful and as I am obliged,

Sir

your very humble

servant Mary Hampson

Be pleased to direct your letter to Mr. George Van Ophoven the younger advocate[2] at Delft for me.

Delft the 1 of August 1680

October 20, 1680:

Sir

At my return to Delft I received the letter you favored me with, but no news of Mr. Franklin to whom I wrote to. I desire that you will do me the favor to let me know what authority is necessary for me to give for I was in so great passion to be out of the place where I had received such barbarous treatment that I gave no order in my business only desired Mr. Franklin to receive the fifty pounds. If he hath not, if I knew what form is to be used I shall do it. I thought if Mr. Franklin received the money and gave his acquittance it would have been enough and the merchants acquittance to Mr. Franklin. I understand nothing of fines[3] which is the reason I am so abused, but I give God thanks that I can suffer wrong rather than do any which is the satisfaction of

Sir

your most humble servant and much

obliged client Mary Hampson.

Delft the 20 de October

[postscript:]

If there be any way to receive my money here I would pay the third part of my alimony so much I abhor the place where that monster of ingratitude does abide, for besides the duty he owes to God as a husband he is obliged to me for the releasing of my jointure and other obligations which my duty did not oblige me to, only my kindness to him, that he might not perish knowing him to be a man of no parts and by consequence the most contemptible of men without fortune and I feared too weak to support the disgrace which attends the want of fortune. You see Doctor how he requites the consideration I had for him. I think it will be necessary for me to put the case, as it is betwixt Mr. Hampson and my self, in print in all countries that the world may know the true reasons of our difference.[4]

November 25, 1680:

Sir

I believe you have not received the second letter I troubled you with. This is to beg the favor of you that you will speak to Mr. Exton[5] to know if Mr. Hampson will pay the fifty pounds to Mr. Franklin as was ordered by the court and the other quarter due the 8 of September last. If he will pay or the court will force him to it I shall write to Mr. Franklin and desire him to pay it to a merchant to be returned to me. If there is nothing to be done in my absence favor me so much as to let me know and I shall give you no further trouble until the spring at which time with God's help I shall come for England. I have written two letters to Mr. Franklin but receiving no answer I take the liberty to write to you hoping you will excuse the trouble from

Sir

your most humble and

obliging servant

Mary Hampson

Delft the 25 November 1680.

Address your letter if you please there Mr. Van Ophoven advocate at Delft.

January 24, 1681:

Sir

I have sent a letter of attorney for one Mr. Jackson a merchant in London[6] if the said man comes to speak with you pray give him an account of my business for I doubt not but Mr. Hampson will give him an answer that may dissuade him from doing me that good office and likewise that you will do what can be done in the court if occasion be and I shall do what is on my part to do. This is all the trouble at present from

Sir

your very much

obliged and most humble

servant Mary Hampson

[postscript]

Send your letters for me to Mr. Jackson if he comes to wait on you if not to be delivered to Mr. Panser merchant, Amsterdam upon the Herring-flete. He is the man by whom I sent the letter of attorney.

April 4, 1681:

Rotterdam the 4 of April

Sir

This gentleman whom does me the kindness to bring this letter to your hand can testify that I am Mrs. Hampson he having seen me with my husband that was in England. I say that was for I am well informed that he is and hath been married a considerable time to an other[7] by which I am free before God but I know it will be hard for to prove it, neither should I desire it, for I seek not his life but would be free before the world as I am before God from the time that he turned me off without showing any just cause and God knows there was not any, yet I was contented for to give him his liberty to live by himself and take a small allowance and let him grow great with my fortune. But since all that I can do will not assuage his malice I have still the right of a wife and if my judges will not oblige him to pay me I desire you will let me know by letter in what manner I must proceed for I can no longer live as a slave. If you think good to write I shall be obliged to you direct your letter to Mr. Henry Goddeus[8] bookseller in Rotterdam. I hope still that God will not harden all men's hearts and that some will seek to do me justice. His [God's] will be done, I am

Sir

Your most humble servant Mary Hampson

May 9, 1681:

Sir

There is one Mr. Gellson that does solicit[9] for me. I desire that you will direct him what is to be done in my business that my alimony be so settle that I may have no more the trouble I have had this 12 years or that I begin my affairs anew for I am out of patience that I can have no rest, for I cannot live in England upon so small a sum yearly nor here unless it be well and quarterly paid. I hope that you will do what the law will allow if Mr. Hampson would consent upon an agreement that we may be the one and other as if we never had seen one another, I am content so that he will give me parte of my estate for I do so abhor his injustice that I do desire since his last cruel usage of me never more to see his face. If you can do my business in my absence I shall give order to Mr. Jackson who hath my letter of attorney to present to you what shall be due to your merit that not in my poor capacity.[10] If my presence is absolutely necessary do me the favor to let me know. I am sir your servant Mary Hampson.

If you please to give your letter to Mr. Gellson or direct it to Rotterdam to Monsieur Godicus, printer in the port.

June 5, 1681:

Rotterdam June the 5 1681

Sir

About six weeks since or more there went from hence to London one Mr. Gellson an English man and because he knew me I desired him to do me the favor to let Mr. Hampson know I was alive and that he would likewise deliver a letter from me to you and one to Sir Richard Lloyd[11] which he said he would do, but since having received letters from the said Mr. Gellson in which he says that Sir Richard Lloyd hath taken great pains in my business but speaks not a word of you in whom I have much confidence for which cause as also not having any answer from you I write this to desire you to let me know what hath been done in court for me for the said Mr. Gellson writes me word that Sir Richard Lloyd must have 8 guineas and that the other charges come to 12 pounds more which

I understand not for I gave no further commission to Mr. Gellson whom I know only by sight than to deliver my letters to you and Sir Richard Lloyd, he being a man that said he knew me by having many years since seen me with Mr. Hampson and that his evidence would take away the pretence whether I was living or not, and if he was capable and faithful in soliciting for me I should pay him, but I have no account from him of any thing that is done for me. He writes me word that Mr. Hampson will pay the money due if I send a letter of attorney signed and sealed in the presence of Mr. Dorvill who now belongs to Mr. Sidney[12] the said Mr. Dorvill's wife[13] is cousin germane[14] to Mr. Hampson's sister married to Ashfield the painter[15] but I think it not necessary to send any more letters of attorney for that [letter] to Mr. Jackson is as good as any other can be and it is signed by Mr. Gellson. Therefore I see Mr. Hampson will never pay me as the agreement obliges him, for if I count the trouble and charge I have no alimony. If you can put me in a way so that the agreement may be nulled or that it be paid according to justice for there is no judge but must give me my charges[16] that Mr. Hampson in malice puts me to and as they well see. If there be any way in law to bring my business to the point it was when I was betrayed to an agreement or to oblige him to return me part of my estate back I would give a considerable part of what I shall receive to the person that was the instrument to accomplish it. Pray let me have your advice in a letter for if it was possible I would have a little rest before I go hence and be no more seen. I employ persons of several judgments to find where is the faithful man that is a lover of truth and justice in hopes of an answer from you I rest

Sir

Your humble

Servant

Mary Hampson

Pray let me know if Mr. Jackson the merchant that hath my letter of attorney hath been with you. I will pay above my condition to have my business done. But if just it be done if you think good to move the court and if they will not just let me know.

NOTES

INTRODUCTION

1. See Lena Cowen Orlin, *Locating Privacy in Tudor London* (Oxford: Oxford University Press, 2007).

2. See Elizabeth Foyster, *Marital Violence: An England Family History, 1660–1857* (Cambridge: Cambridge University Press, 2005).

3. See Laura Gowing, *Domestic Dangers: Women, Words, and Sex in Early Modern London* (Oxford: Oxford University Press, 1996).

4. The only exception to this was freehold land (land not held through long-term or "life" leases). Although the wife could not claim the income from such land during her marriage, she could receive it in her widowhood. Also, the husband could not sell this property without his wife's consent—though this created another potential conflict in a marriage.

5. Robert Callis, *The Case and Argument Against Sir Ignoramus of Cambridge* (London, 1648), 21.

6. In many European countries a married woman maintained some legal rights to her property, and in cases where the marriage broke down she could be awarded a separate estate solely for her use. Conversely, in England unmarried women had a legal standing unprecedented in Europe as legal individuals in their own right with no requirements to have a male guardian. Approximately 50 percent of women in England were unmarried at a given time in the period. See Amy M. Froide, *Never Married: Singlewomen in Early Modern England* (Oxford: Oxford University Press, 2005).

7. See Amy Louise Erickson, "Coverture and Capitalism," *History Workshop Journal* 59 (2005): 4.

8. Robert Bruce, *The Way to True Peace and Rest* (London, 1617), 294.

9. Edward Reyner, *Considerations Concerning Marriage* (London, 1657), 14. The metaphor of the mother hen protecting her chicks under her wings is found in the gospel of Matthew 23:37 and Luke 13:34, creating an analogy between the husband and Christ.

10. Ibid., 13.

11. Ibid., 24.

12. John Fletcher, *Rule a Wife and Have a Wife*, in *The Dramatic Works in the Beaumont and Fletcher Canon*, ed. Fredson Bowers, vol. 6 (Cambridge, Cambridge University Press, 1985) 3.5.90–92. This play was first performed in 1624 and remained a favorite with theatergoers well into the nineteenth century.

13. William Shakespeare, *Taming of the Shrew*, in *Complete Works*, ed. Jonathan Bates and Eric Rasmussen (2007), 5.1.176.

14. See Pamela Allen Brown, *Better a Shrew Than a Sheep: Women, Drama, and the Culture of Jest in Early Modern England* (Ithaca, NY: Cornell University Press, 2003).

15. Tim Stretton, *Marital Litigation in the Court of Requests 1542–1642* (Cambridge: Cambridge University Press, 2008), 205.

16. Anne Clifford, *The Diary of Anne Clifford*, ed. Katherine O. Acheson (Toronto: Broadview, 2007), 111–112, 141.

17. Letter from Anne Clifford to Francis Russell, January 14, 1638, MS Harley 7001, f. 144, British Library, London.

18. Anne Wentworth, *A Vindication of Anne Wentworth* (London, 1677), 4. This pamphlet, though quite different in tone and context, may have provided one model for Mary Hampson's own pamphlet of marital abuse.

19. Mary Cuthbertson, *Sir Lyon Pilkington, Barronet, Appellant, Mary Cuthbertson, widow, Respondent: The Respondent's Case* (London, 1711).

20. *The Case betwixt Thornton Cage and his Wife* (London, 1684).

21. These courts began as petitions to the Lord Chancellor of England asking for the redress of wrongs. They were later merged with the existing legal system, running in tandem with common law courts. See Tim Stretton, *Women Waging Law in Elizabethan England* (Cambridge: Cambridge University Press, 1998).

22. *A Letter to a Person of Quality, Occasioned by a Printed Libel Entitled: "The cause of the difference between Tobias Cage esquire, and Mary his wife"* (London, 1678).

23. Stretton, *Marital Litigation*, 193.

24. Ibid., 172.

25. *A Vindication of the Earl of Anglesey* (London, 1702); *The Case of Angela Marguerita Cottington* (London, 1680).

26. Robert Brook, *The Reading of that Famous Lawyer, Sr. Robert Brook* (London, 1647), 117.

27. These include a long list of marital guides, among them John Dod and Richard Clever, *A Godly form of Householde Government* (London, 1612); William Gouge, *Of Domesticall Duties* (London, 1622); Nathaniel Hardy, *Love and Fear the Inseperable Twins of a Blest Matrimony* (London, 1653); and Edward Reyner, *Considerations Concerning Marriage the Honour, duties, Benefits, Troubles of it* (1657).

28. Thomas Bentley, *Fifth Lamp of Virginitie* (London, 1582), 75.

29. Foyster, *Marital Violence*, 99.

30. Mary Aubrey Montagu was also a childhood friend of the poet Katherine Philips. Philips wrote a number of poems and letters to Mary Montagu, whom she

called Rosania in her poetry. Mary Montagu reportedly "cradled" Philips in her arms when Philips died.

31. Margaret Cunningham, *A Pairt of the Life of Lady Margaret Cuninghame*, ed. C. K. Sharpe (Edinburgh, 1827).

32. The Inner Temple is one of the four Inns of Court where lawyers in seventeenth-century England received legal training. Many lawyers retained chambers within the Inns of Court, where they conducted their business and also sometimes lived.

33. Sergeants at Law were the only lawyers allowed to serve as judges and had important, and at times exclusive, rights in the common law courts, and preferential rights in other courts.

34. Some of Robert Hampson's buildings survive, including no. 9 along the King's Bench Walk in the Inner Temple, London. Robert Hampson is also buried in the Inner Temple church. See Chapter Two for a discussion of the destruction of Hampson's building no. 8 on the King's Bench Walk.

35. Robert agreed to this trip at the time.

36. Letters from Mary Hampson to William Trumbull (1680–1681) MS D/ED/O53, Berkshire Records Office, Reading, UK. Spelling and punctuation have been modernized in all quotations from these letters throughout this book.

37. A fictitious plot to murder Charles II that nevertheless resulted in arrests and executions.

38. One copy is held in the University Library, Cambridge, shelfmark Syn.5.68.36. Another is held in the Bodleian Library, Oxford, shelfmark C 11.1(7) Linc. The third copy is privately owned by the editor. The Bodleian Library copy is from a second printing and includes an additional page at the end of the pamphlet.

39. No copies of Mary Cage's pamphlet have survived. We have only Tobias's rebuttal.

40. This single remaining copy of Robert Hampson's pamphlet was held in the Guildhall Library, London. It was destroyed in a bombing raid in December 1940; the library was hit and approximately twenty-five thousand books were destroyed.

41. This second edition is dated 1684 as well, but this is not to preclude the possibility that it was printed in 1685. It was common for printers to retain the same date, making as few changes as possible to the cover page in subsequent editions.

A PLAIN *and* COMPENDIOUS RELATION *of the* CASE *of* MRS. MARY HAMPSON . . .

1. Sir Nicholas Pedley was a serjeant at law, and also a member of Parliament for Huntingdon.

2. Samuel Pont was twice mayor of the Borough of Huntingdon.

3. These bonds were documents confirming moneys owed to the bearer. They were originally Elizabeth Wingfield's and Mary managed to take them away from her

mother's room before Elizabeth died. Money was payable according to the conditions stated in the bond.

4. A nuncupative will was made verbally by dying people who were too ill to sign their name. These wills had to be verified by two witnesses. Mary suggests here that her mother never made this nuncupative will. However, it was legally accepted and Robert did sell land belonging to Elizabeth Wingfield using this will.

5. When Mary says the maid was of no credit she means the maid had a poor reputation and would not be seen as a reliable witness in court had the will been challenged.

6. Mary's statement here is corroborated by a deed of sale for a house owned by Elizabeth Wingfield and sold by Robert Hampson in December 1670.

7. Unless otherwise modified, the word *town* refers to London.

8. Here she refers to the last house she and Robert leased before the end of their marriage in the New Southampton Buildings near what is now Bloomsbury Square. A number of houses that Mary would have known still border the square.

9. The Inner Temple.

10. Mary's marriage portion—that is, the documents that stipulated the agreement entered into by Robert Hampson by which certain houses and properties were settled on Mary during her life should she outlive her husband.

11. The *London Gazette*. See note 134.

12. She names this person later in the pamphlet, where she expands on this episode. He was Charles le Gard, who lived at Somerset House. See notes 133 and 136.

13. The discovery that the lands settled on Mary as part of her jointure—or marriage portion—were already mortgaged or "engaged by recognisance" and thus unlikely to provide a secure income for Mary should Robert die was the catalyst for the many marital disputes that followed.

14. The fenlands were large tracts of marshy land in Cambridgeshire and Huntingdonshire. In the seventeenth century the Bedford Levels project attempted to drain the fens and bring them into agricultural production. At the beginning of the project, investors, including Robert Hampson's father, believed they would make a profit through the purchase of this cheap marsh land soon to become rich agricultural land, but this proved not to be the case. Robert Hampson would take an active part in this project for decades. The Fen Office was housed at his chambers in Tanfield Court in the Inner Temple from 1657 until the Great fire of 1666, when they were destroyed. He rebuilt chambers in Tanfield court, and the lease for number 3 was purchased from Robert Hampson to house the Fen Office in 1667. At his death, he still owned land in Raveley Fen. The fenland property he owned never made a profit and contributed to his financial and marital difficulties alike.

15. Chatteris, Huntingdonshire.

16. The manor of Taplow was purchased by Thomas Hampson (Robert's father) in 1635 and was later sold by Robert's nephew, Dennis Hampson, in about 1700. There is

evidence in the will of Thomas Hampson that he did leave much of his movable property to Robert Hampson, including his cattle, linen, plate, "household stuff," furniture, sums of money, and his London house in Holborn street. Robert was also granted the administration of Sir Thomas's estate jointly with his younger brother Ambrose.

17. Mary could be referring here to Katherine Hampson, who would later raise Mary's eldest daughter, Elizabeth, and leave Elizabeth the bulk of her estate upon her death in 1678. The other sisters could have been Rebecca, who married Ambrose Benet, and/or Margaret, who married Sir Giles Hungerford. In 1660 four of Robert Hampson's siblings sued Robert for money he owed them.

18. According to Katherine Hampson's will, Robert Hampson owed her three hundred pounds in 1678.

19. Mary gave birth to her son Robert, who died in infancy.

20. Mary refers here to her financial safety.

21. Sir John Glynn, Lord Chief Justice 1655–1660.

22. A fine was a financial obligation. Mary signed a document that said she would sign away her rights to her jointure when she turned twenty-one. It is unclear how legal such a document signed in these circumstances would be.

23. This refers to lands and a house in Huntingdonshire in the towns of Bury and Wistow. This property would be involved in long-running disputes that would continue after the deaths of both Mary and Robert.

24. A feoffee was a trustee responsible for the holding of land for the benefit of another person.

25. Henry Poulton was a member of Lincoln's Inn, one of the Inns of Court. He also had a house and property in Twickenham near London. He appears often as a close associate of Robert Hampson in both the pamphlet and the legal documents relating to the marriage dispute. Robert was named as one of the executors of his estate after Poulton's death.

26. A first cousin.

27. This may be Sir John Holland (c. 1603–1701) of Quiddenham, Norfolk.

28. Mary is referring here to Robert's legal work on one of the six regional law circuits of the Assizes, courts held twice a year throughout England. Lawyers from London were sent out "on circuit" to preside as judges in these courts. They were first set up so that people did not have to go to London and could instead have their cases heard in their own area.

29. This was a medieval barony made after the Norman Conquest. At the time Mary wrote this, the honor of Clare was in the possession of Sir John Holland, the same man who leased Robert's Holborn house. It was common for landowners to employ men with a legal background to manage the financial concerns of their properties, as Robert does here.

30. She was pregnant with her daughter Anne.

31. This child was her daughter Mary, born in January 1662.

32. Mary confuses the day of the week but otherwise gives an accurate account of the order issued on July 22, 1661. Robert Hampson's father, Sir Thomas Hampson, was Clerk of the Statutes office between 1634 and 1640. Apparently Sir Thomas illegally kept the Statutes Books for those years in his possession. The period between 1640 and 1660 was a very unsettled time in England because of the civil wars, and this is likely why no one came looking for these books until after the Restoration of Charles II in 1660.

33. Adrian and Richard May were granted the office of Clerk of the Statutes after Thomas Hampson. It is unclear whether Mary is referring to Adrian or Richard.

34. Blows directed at the breasts, genitals, and womb were often reported in marriage disputes.

35. Sir John Hinton was a physician to Charles II, and admitted as an Honorary Fellow of the College of Physicians in 1664. Hinton was called in by Charles I's queen Henrietta Maria at the birth of her daughter Henrietta.

36. Doctor Thomas Nurse ran a successful practice in Westminster, especially after the Restoration. Mary later comments that he had also been doctor to her father and other Wingfields.

37. Medicine.

38. Diseases of the lung.

39. Addressed. This statement is supposed to convey to the reader that Robert Hampson actively participated in the preparations for Mary's trip to France and thus had clearly agreed she could go. This was important to her claims that she traveled with his permission and was not a runaway.

40. Rye is located in Sussex, twenty-seven miles from Dover; it is one of the Cinque Ports. In the seventeenth century its importance as a port had greatly diminished; this was due to the silting of the harbor and the increasing reliance on deep water ports for larger trading vessels. Despite this, Rye continued to be a popular point of embarkation for passengers traveling to the continent.

41. If Mary were a runaway her rights to jointure would be void and Robert could sell the property contained in the jointure more easily.

42. This is a reference to the Great Plague of 1665–66, and one of Mary's few references to contemporary events.

43. Charenton-le-Pont is a southeastern suburb of Paris, where the Seine and Marne rivers join. The area housed an important Protestant community in the seventeenth century.

44. A "feoffee in trust" held land and the income produced from it (or other assets) for the benefit of another individual. This was a legal device often used to provide an income for a woman who was separated from her husband. Legally speaking, even the goods she purchased with money provided in this way could not be taken by the husband because they were, in legal terms, the property of the executors of the trust.

45. Bankers.

46. Robert Hampson was admitted to his chambers on February 20, 1647, located underneath the library, 1 Tanfield Court.

47. A personal agreement between the two.

48. These were all likely designed to entrap Mary. The borrowing of money by a wife without the consent of her husband would create a justification for the husband to ask for a separation without paying the wife maintenance. The admission by a wife that she had run away would have the same effect. Clearly, at this point in her life Mary was not quite so naïve as Robert hoped. What Mary was hoping to do by returning to Robert was reestablish her marital rights—that is, the right to maintenance both during her husband's life and after his death. She also may have been attempting to reunite with her children, who were at this point living with relatives.

49. Holman and Edwards were members of the Inner Temple. Edwards served on a variety of Inner Temple administrative committees with Robert Hampson and would appear several times supporting him in his marital disputes with Mary.

50. Sir John Maynard was an eminent and important lawyer and politician in the seventeenth century. After the Restoration of Charles II, he served as the king's lawyer.

51. Mary's decision to move into Robert's chambers meant she was surrounded by men who were her husband's professional colleagues and often personal friends. In the Inner Temple she could not rely on her neighbors to intervene for her during Robert's abuse.

52. Mr. Powell, an Inner Temple lawyer, often supported Robert in his marital disputes with Mary. Interestingly, Powell also appears in another pamphlet account of marital discord, *The cause of the difference between Tobias Cage esquire, and Mary his wife...* (London, 1678). In this pamphlet, Tobias Cage names Powell as acting for Cage's wife both professionally and personally. In this account, Cage insinuates that Powell is unprincipled as Powell supports Mary Cage in a variety of dishonest ploys to extract money from Cage, and to discredit him.

53. Hopton Shuter served on several Inner Temple committees with Robert Hampson. Like Powell, Poulton, Edwards, and Holman, Shuter often appears in documents related to the Hampson marital dispute as Robert's supporter.

54. Bedlam was a popular name for Bethlehem Hospital in London; it housed mainly the insane in the 1660s.

55. A method of securing a person's arms and legs in a stretched-out position in preparation for whipping.

56. Community interference in domestic affairs was considered appropriate.

57. Hopton Shuter had chambers in Fig Tree Court, in the Inner Temple.

58. These were selected members of the Inner Temple responsible for administration and compliance with Inner Temple rules. In January 1668, when these events occurred, several of Hampson's close associates were Officers of the House.

59. She refers here to the ecclesiastical Court of Arches.

60. John Fountaine was another prominent lawyer and a close associate of Sir John Maynard. He was a distant relation of Mary's and often interceded for her during her marital difficulties. Unfortunately, he died in 1671 before these were resolved.

61. An Inn of Chancery, which housed offices for lawyers at this time.

62. A fabric of thick wool or silk that was used for clothing and upholstery.

63. Sarah Whalley was the wife of John Whalley. She died in December 1663.

64. Mary's depositions in the Court of Arches and High Court of Delegates cases offer different versions of her conflict with her mother, including accusations that the crux of their disagreement was that Mary had become a Catholic. Certainly the situation was more complicated than Mary presents here.

65. A form of hysteria believed to be related to female reproductive organs. Mary may also have believed herself to be pregnant at this time. Note here Mary contradicts her earlier account of her estrangement with her mother.

66. Doctor Thomas Willis was an eminent physician who was consulted by the Duke of York, brother to Charles II, and his family. He lived in St. Martin's Lane, as did Mary's mother at this time, and thus would have been a convenient person to consult.

67. She refers to the minister here.

68. Here Mary says she did not receive communion according to the Rites of the Church of England. She says this was because she did not feel spiritually prepared. The reason she feels the need to explain her refusal to take communion is because Roman Catholics often refused to take communion according to the Rites of the Church of England. In court depositions Robert Hampson accuses Mary of being a Roman Catholic. At this time, there was a great deal of prejudice and animosity toward Roman Catholics in England.

69. A waxed cloth used for wrapping corpses.

70. The Archbishop of Canterbury and the ecclesiastical courts, or the Lord Chancellor and the civil courts.

71. See note 5 above.

72. The provincial courts of Canterbury and York exercised jurisdiction over matters concerning people whose estates upon their death were over a certain amount, or who were from certain social groups. A copy of Mary Wingfield's nuncupative will can still be seen in the wills of the Prerogative Court of Canterbury (now held in the National Archives, London), where it was proved without any investigation.

73. Sir John Fiennes served as a colonel in Cromwell's army and was the brother of Nathaniel Fiennes, fourth Viscount Saye and Sele.

74. This maid was Katherine Browne, who was sent by Robert Hampson to Bridewell prison on a charge of theft and was whipped.

75. A Theodore Deveaux is recorded as a physician to Queen Catherine and was

knighted in January 1666. In 1664 he resided at St. Paul's, Covent Garden. Deveaux is also listed as a trustee of a freehold property in St. James Square in 1673, along with a Robert Grayden, who may have been related to the maid Mary called "Mr. Hampson's creature" earlier in the story, also called Graden.

76. These men, as noted previously, appear regularly in documents related to the Hampson marital difficulties and were clearly supportive of Robert.

77. The office of the Six Clerks kept the records for business that had been authorized by the king and other business related to the Court of Chancery. The office was located in Chancery Lane, at the Holborn end. Apparently there were also residences there.

78. The "Spiritual Court" Mary refers to here is the Court of Arches, the ecclesiastical court that dealt with matrimonial matters. Prior to the Great Fire of 1666 the court sat in the church of St. Mary de Arcubus or Bow Church. From October 1666 to April 1672 it sat in Exeter House. Thus, the Hampson case was heard at Exeter House, which coincidentally was where Robert was also residing at the time.

79. Sir Giles Sweit, was Regius Professor of Civil Law at Oxford and, after 1660, Dean of the Court of Arches.

80. Doctor Richard Ball was master of the Inner Temple church. He was appointed master on February 2, 1661. He also performed the marriage ceremony for Mary's daughter Elizabeth Hampson and Charles Bill in 1681.

81. Mary consistently shows in this pamphlet and her court depositions and statements that she has some understanding of the law.

82. In the High Court of Delegates.

83. In the Restoration, the state of excommunication did not carry with it the stigma or punitive sanctions it once had.

84. Sir Walter Walker was a judge of the Court of Admiralty and also served as one of King Charles II's lawyers.

85. Although Mary may have wished to open Robert up to the scorn of his peers in the legal profession, the court would be more interested in brokering a settlement. Early settlement in a marriage dispute was encouraged, and often brought about by formal or informal arbitration, as appears to be the case here.

86. Robert asserts that Mary is dead in a lawsuit he brought against Mary's cousin, John Whalley, in 1674.

87. Laurence Debusty (or Debussy) was a merchant in London and is mentioned in Samuel Pepys's diary on September 14, 1665.

88. Anne Geneviève, the Duchess of Longueville, was the only daughter of Henri II de Bourbon, Prince of Condé, and his wife Charlotte-Marguerite de Montmorency. By the 1670s, when Mary was in Paris, the Duchess was nearing the end of her life and was devoted to religion and good works. High-status French women would often support abused wives and women in distress.

89. She was probably related to Charles de La Porte, Duc de Meilleraye (1602–

1664). It is likely that Mary served as a waiting gentlewoman or some type of upper servant in this house, given her financial situation.

90. Simon Arnauld de Pomponne was the French Secretary of State for Foreign Affairs from 1671–1679.

91. Charles Colbert, Marquis de Croissy, was ambassador to England from 1668 to 1674 and negotiated the first treaty of Dover with King Charles II in 1670.

92. Mary Aubrey Montagu was the second wife of William Montagu, Chief Baron of the Exchequer, who was a distant relation of Mary Hampson. In 1669 Mary Montagu arbitrated a short-lived settlement between Robert and Mary Hampson. She was also likely the "Friend" Mary addresses at the beginning of the pamphlet. Mary Montagu would continue to help Mary into the 1690s. Mary Montagu is best known as the poet Katherine Philips's friend. She is addressed as "Rosania" in Philip's poetry.

93. Louis XIV of France.

94. Charles II of England.

95. This sentence is quite awkward, but essentially it says she was forced in 1678 to return to England to seek her alimony.

96. This is likely Sir Richard Lloyd (1634–1686), Dean of the Court of Arches from 1684 to 1686.

97. Mary was back in England by February 1678, though she remained for only a short period before returning to the continent.

98. She refers here to the delegates who heard her case in the High Court of Delegates.

99. Common lawyers made up the commission in most cases by the end of the seventeenth century, though bishops and peers could also sit on commissions. However those involved—the appellants and respondents—could only suggest the type of commission they would prefer, and whether they wished it to include civilians and/or common lawyers. It was the Lord Chancellor who made the choice of the judge-delegates in the end. In 1671 this would have been Sir Orlando Bridgeman. It is unlikely he would have loaded the commission with Robert Hampson's friends, though given Robert's professional status, and the all-male environment of the court, Mary may well have felt intimidated.

100. In other words, they died and thus, Mary believed, came face to face with divine judgment.

101. A proctor is a lawyer. Mary complains that Robert Hampson's lawyer was the brother of one of the judges.

102. Mammon or wealth.

103. The Hampsons make a short appearance in Edmund Everard's *The Depositions and Examinations of Mr. Edmund Everard . . . Concerning the Horrid Popish Plot* (London, 1679). See Chapter Two.

104. Sir Thomas Exton (1631–1680) served as a judge of the Admiralty Court and Dean of the Court of Arches. Thomas Pinfold was an ecclesiastical lawyer.

105. A sign of disrespect.

106. An apparition or ghost.

107. Several Robinsons are record as being admitted to the Inner Temple during this period.

108. Francis Burke states in a legal document that from June 1683 through November 1684 Robert refused to pay him Mary's alimony on her behalf and put him to some trouble.

109. In a letter to Sir William Trumbull in October 1680 Mary wrote that she thought it might be necessary to publish her story of marital wrong. It is likely she wrote the account sometime in 1681–82 and that it was printed in 1682.

110. Henry Goddaeus, called Mr. Henricus Goddeus in Mary's letters to William Trumbull, was a Rotterdam printer who had a shop in the Newstreet, 3 Rotterdam. He printed *The Rotterdam's Courant*, a newssheet which was reprinted in England by Benjamin Harris. Goddaeus also printed Katherine Sutton's *A Christian Womans Experiences of the Glorious Working of Gods Free Grace* (Rotterdam, 1663) among many other books. Goddaeus was active in Rotterdam from 1663 to 1682; his widow took over the printing house from 1684 to 1690.

111. Everard knew the book traders and printers in the Netherlands. He did not arrive in the Netherlands until 1682, which more firmly places publication date for the first edition in 1682. Everard was serving as a government informer at this time.

112. Unfortunately Mary was in error here. Desertion was not grounds for anything more than a separation from bed and board.

113. Appear like a gentlewoman of a good family.

114. Mary was seventeen when she was married to Robert Hampson.

115. Robert Hampson's family home was in Taplow, Buckinghamshire.

116. A gentleman.

117. "Oficious" is used here to mean actively serving the required purpose.

118. This was the son of Robert's sister Mary and Sir John Laurence, second Baronet of Iver. Thomas Laurence became the third Baronet of Iver.

119. A receipt for the money. Laurence asks Mary to sign a document saying she had received the money before she actually received it. Laurence may have genuinely felt this would be the best way to convince Robert to send the alimony, as Robert would then have a receipt to prove it, and not have to worry about more requests being made for the same amount; or this could have been yet another ploy to swindle Mary.

120. In 1673 Everard admitted to participating in a plot to poison the Duke of Monmouth, though he later claimed this was after being threatened with torture on the rack. In his pamphlet on the Popish Plot in 1679, he accuses Mary Hampson and others of spreading this lie to cover their own crimes. Everard became a government spy in the 1680s and was sent to the Netherlands.

121. Elizabeth Hamilton, Countess de Gramont, was the daughter of Sir George

Hamilton and Mary Butler. She married Philibert, Count de Gramont. They lived in France from 1664.

122. The book of charms that Everard tries to impress Mary with was a popular and widely available French *grimoire* or spell book, probably written in the sixteenth century, entitled *Enchiridion Leonis Papae serenissimo Imperatori Carolo Magno.* It contains a number of charms to ward off evil and disaster.

123. According to Titus Oates, the man who fabricated the Popish Plot, Everard knew how to make and use fireworks and explosives.

124. A tall tale.

125. The uniform of a household. This would identify Everard as a servant.

126. Everard would soon be arrested in December 1673 on suspicion of planning to poison the Duke of Monmouth, Charles II's illegitimate son.

127. This may be the Colonel Justin Maccarty (also Justin McCarthy, later Lord Montcashel). Everard mentions in his Popish Plot pamphlet that McCarthy was in Paris in 1673. McCarthy likely served in the French regiment of Sir George Hamilton (the father of Elizabeth Hamilton; see note 121).

128. Sir Henry Coventry, appointed Secretary of State in 1672.

129. John Grenville, first earl of Bath.

130. See note 87.

131. A wife was generally allowed the use of one-third of the income of her deceased husband's real estate. Mary signed away this right as part of the agreement reached during the High Court of Delegates case.

132. Mary may not be completely honest here, as she does not mention the free-hold land her uncle John Whalley settled on her. The income from that land in 1674 was £74 a year and was collected by Robert Hampson. At his death the income from this property would revert to her. She alludes to this in her letters to William Trumbull, when she asks if there were any way the income from her own property could be legally sent to her. After Robert's death she sues her daughters to retain control of this property and the income from it. See Chapter Three.

133. Charles le Gard was a groom of the Privy Chamber to Queen Catherine of Braganza.

134. Notice of this event appeared in the *London Gazette* on February 7, 1677 [1678].

135. Sir Richard Elsworth (or Ellsworth) was a gentleman of Charles II's Privy Chamber.

136. Thomas Butler, sixth Earl of Ossory became chamberlain to the queen, Catherine of Braganza, in 1676. Somerset House, where le Gard had chambers, was given to Catherine after the death of Charles II's mother, Henrietta Maria. Although Catherine did not reside there permanently, she kept it staffed. Le Gard's theft would come under the jurisdiction of her chamberlain, Thomas Butler.

137. See the Introduction for a discussion of the editions of this pamphlet, or "book" as Mary calls it.

138. Here she refers to Everard's Popish Plot pamphlet. See note 103.

139. Mary could not put the bill in herself because as a married woman she was still under coverture. It was common in marital disputes for relatives of the wife to take up court action for her.

140. Psalm 119:71.

141. This addition to the second London printing of the pamphlet comes from the High Court of Delegates case.

142. "22 of May, 1671 before the gentlemen Exton, Clark, and Pinfold, delegates in the public court held at Exeter House on the Strand, in the county of Middlesex between the hours of ten and twelve am, Thomas Oughton, Notary Public and others present. Hampson vs Hampson, Exton [and] Franklin."

143. The comment in italics was inserted by Mary and is presented in italics in the pamphlet.

144. The Latin asserts the legal statement above is taken from the actual document and is a "vera copia" or a true account of what the document says and was supplied by Thomas Oughton, registrar of the High Court of Delegates. This was the elder Thomas Oughton who died in 1695. His son, another Thomas Oughton, also served as a registrar of the High Court of Delegates and wrote the *Ordo Judiciorum* concerning the procedures of the ecclesiastical courts.

CHAPTER I

1. Letters from Mary Hampson to William Trumbull, 1680–81, D/ED/O53, Berkshire Records Office, Reading, UK.

2. The manor house at Taplow and the estate surrounding it was entailed on the eldest son, Thomas. An entail was a legal restriction that dictated to whom property could be left.

3. Will of Sir Thomas Hampson, 1655, Prob/11/246, National Archives, London.

4. St. Andrew, Holborn Baptisms, 1654–1676, LMA 6667/4, London Metropolitan Archives.

5. Robert Hampson vs Katherine Hampson, 1659, C 6/42/100; Robert Hampson vs Ambrose, George, Katherine and Margaret Hampson, 1660, C 6/77/30, National Archives, London.

6. Deed of Release, Raveley Fen, 1694, 319/Bundle 15/1, Cambridgeshire Archives, Huntingdon, UK.

7. A legal suit filed by Robert Hampson against John Whalley's executor, a nephew also called John Whalley, suggests that Mary's uncle had initially promised the couple some houses, along with agricultural land. But in his will, John Whalley left Mary only agricultural land. Harpson [Robert Hampson] vs John Whalley, 1664, C 10/103/65, National Archives, London.

8. Harpson [Robert Hampson] vs John Whalley, 1664.

9. See Chapter Three for a discussion of the difficulties Mary had in claiming the income of this property after Robert's death.

10. Robert Hampson vs Katherine Hampson, 1659.

11. Henry II began the custom of having judges "ride circuit" or travel around the country to preside over judicial proceedings. This allowed litigants to have their cases heard at higher courts without the cost of traveling to London. The country was divided into six circuits in the seventeenth century. Robert was "called to the bar" in 1659, so as a senior barrister he was eligible to ride a circuit as a judge.

12. The Rolls of Statutes were a record of statutes or acts passed by Parliament that had been kept since medieval times. They were originally long rolls of parchment stitched together.

13. *Journal of the House of Lords*, vol. 11 (1660–1666), 285–286, 316–317.

14. This incident is told in three places: Mary's pamphlet, and the two court cases. See next note.

15. Hampson vs Hampson, restitution of conjugal rights, 1670, EE 3, Court of Arches, f. 522r, Lambeth Palace Archives, London. This case will be referred to as CA70 in subsequent references, with the folio page number following. Hampson vs Hampson, matrimonial cause: restoration of conjugal rights, High Court of Delegates, 1670, DEL1/110 f. 83r–83v, 144r, National Archives, London. This case will be referred to as HCD70 in subsequent references, with the folio page number following. (*Note:* "r" following the folio page number refers to the right-hand facing page, "v" refers to the opposite or verso side of that page. In manuscript the verso or back of the facing right-hand page is often not numbered, as is the case with both these manuscripts.) The legal format changes Mary's first-person deposition into the third person. Spelling and punctuation has been modernized in all quotations from legal documents throughout this book.

16. See discussion at the beginning of this chapter concerning how individuals told their stories in court settings in order to further their own interests.

17. Susan Scott and Christopher J. Duncan, *Biology of Plagues: Evidence from Historical Populations* (Cambridge: Cambridge University Press, 2001), 258.

18. St John the Baptist (Keyston, Huntingdonshire), north transept, stone slab in floor.

19. HCD70, f. 95v.

20. HCD70, f. 142r.

21. HCD70, f. 134r–135v; CA70 f. 517v–518r.

22. The only exception to this was when the jointure had been secured through an act of Parliament—a course only the wealthiest and most aristocratic of families could afford to take.

23. HCD70, f. 175r–176v; CA70, f. 518v–519r.

24. HCD70, f. 176r; CA70, f. 518r.

25. CA70, f. 541r; HCD70, f. 176v–177r.

26. HCD70, f. 98v–99r.

27. Gwynne Kennedy, *Just Anger: Representing Women's Anger in Early Modern England* (Carbondale: Southern Illinois University Press, 2000).

28. John Strype, *A Survey of The Cities of London and Westminster* (London, 1720), 84.

29. CA70, 511v.

30. Will of Elizabeth Wingfield (nuncupative), 1669, Prob/11/331, National Archives, London.

31. "Sale to Martin Buck," St. Edward's Parish Deeds, 1670, CCCC 09/09/124, Corpus Christi College Library and Archives, Cambridge, UK.

32. HCD70, f. 154r.

33. HCD70, f. 183r.

34. HCD70, f. 154v.

35. HCD70, f. 155v.

36. HCD70, f. 183r.

37. Chambers Admissions Book, 1615–1667, CHAM 1/2, Inner Temple Archives, London.

38. It was not uncommon for people to air their grievances in print during the period, and there was a good market for these pamphlets by a public that then, as now, enjoyed reading scandal.

39. Tobias Cage, *A Letter to a Person of Quality, Occasioned by a Printed Libel, Entituled, "The Cause of the Difference Between Tobias Cage esquire, and Mary his wife"* (London, 1678).

40. The Court of Requests was one of the courts of equity that would at times hear cases regarding marital disputes in the late sixteenth and early seventeenth centuries. Elizabeth Garth's suit was brought on her behalf by her father, Sir Benjamin Tichbourne.

41. Tim Stretton, *Marital Litigation in the Court of Requests* (Cambridge: Cambridge University Press, 2008), 205.

42. Margaret Cunningham, *A Pairt of the Life of Lady Margaret Cuninghame*, ed. C. K. Sharpe (Edinburgh, 1837), 5.

43. Joanne Bailey, " 'I dye [sic] by Inches:' Locating Wife Beating in the Concept of a Privatization of Marriage and Violence in Eighteenth-century England," 31, no. 3 (2006): 281. See also Walton vs Walton, DDR/EJ/PRC/2/1718/13, 1718, University of Durham, Durham, UK.

44. HCD70, f. 102r–103v.

45. Edmund Ashfield was a gentleman painter who was also a member of Lincoln's Inn. He was a student of Michael Wright and worked in both oil and crayon. He is credited with several portraits, including a pastel of Queen Catherine of Braganza. *Oxford Dictionary of National Biography*, 2004–2013, s.v. "Edmund Ashfield."

46. Doreen M. Slatter, "Records of the Court of Arches," *Journal of Ecclesiastical History* 4 (1953): 147.

CHAPTER 2

1. Letter from Mary Hampson to William Trumbull, August 9, 1680, D/ED/O53, Berkshire Records Office, Reading, UK.

2. Deposition of Francis Burke, Hampson vs. Hampson, 1684, Del 2/35, National Archives, London.

3. Edmund Everard, *The Depositions and Examinations of Mr. Edmund Everard . . . Concerning the Horrid Popish Plot* (London, 1679) 14.

4. Martin Ingram, *Church Courts, Sex and Marriage in England, 1570–1640* (Cambridge: Cambridge University Press, 1987), 342; G.I.O. Duncan, *The High Court of Delegates* (Cambridge: Cambridge University Press, 1971), 82, 12.

5. See the many entries on Robert Hampson in F. A. Inderwick, ed., *Calendar of the Inner Temple Records*, vol. 3 (London, 1901).

6. Amy Louise Erickson, *Women and Property in Early Modern England* (London: Routledge, 1993) 113.

7. Deposition of Francis Burke, 1684.

8. Letters from Mary Hampson to William Trumbull (1680–81). See Appendix.

9. Mary relates this episode in greater detail in the second half of her pamphlet when she describes her attempts to collect her alimony.

10. See William Heale, *The Great Advocate and Oratour for Women or the Arraignment, Tryall and Conviction of all Such Wicked Husbands or Monsters* (London, 1682).

11. It is possible that this person was Thomas Robson, Trumbull's solicitor, who acted for him when he was ambassador to France in 1685–86; see Ruth Clark, *William Trumbull in Paris 1685–1686* (Cambridge: Cambridge University Press, 1938), 100.

12. Letter from Mary Hampson to William Trumbull, June 5, 1681.

13. See Bernard Capp, "Bigamous Marriage in Early Modern England," *Historical Journal* 52.3 (2009): 537–556.

14. This was one of the few exceptions under coverture where a woman's property did not pass automatically to the husband on marriage. The husband could use the income from the freehold property, and all management remained in his hands during the marriage, but he could not sell it or give it away in his will. On his death, the property returned to the wife. Should the wife die before the husband, the freehold property was supposed to descend to the heirs appointed in the original will, in this case Elizabeth and Mary Hampson.

15. The court papers connected to this dispute are Harpson [Robert Hampson] vs John Whalley, 1664, C 10/103/65; and Elizabeth and Mary Hampson vs John Whalley, 1674, C 5/610/78, National Archives, London.

16. Everard, *Popish Plot*, 14.

17. For detailed discussions of the murderous wife, see Laura Gowing, *Domestic Dangers*; and Francis Dolan, *Dangerous Familiars*, in Suggested Readings.

18. For an account of another of Everard's victims, see Robert Walsh, *The True State, Case, and Condition of Sir Robert Walsh, Knight* (Amsterdam, 1687).

19. Everard, *Popish Plot*, 14–15.

20. Paul Gerardus Hoftijzer and C. C. Barfoot, *Fabrics and Fabrication: The Myth and Making of William and Mary* (Rodopi, 1990), 85; Alan Marshall, *Intelligence and Espionage in the Reign of Charles II, 1660–1685* (Cambridge: Cambridge University Press, 2003), 276.

21. Marshall, *Intelligence and Espionage*, 276.

22. Inderwick, *Calendar*, 87.

23. Ibid., 195–198.

24. Response of Mary Hampson (daughter), Mary Hampson vs. Charles and Elizabeth Bill, and Mary Hampson, 1694, C 5/164/50, National Archives, London.

25. It also indicates that those who oversaw the Inner Temple church either did not know or did not care that Robert had been excommunicated, which status should have made burial in this church impossible.

CHAPTER 3

1. Mary Hampson vs. Charles and Elizabeth Bill, and Mary Hampson, 1693, C 5/109/21, National Archives, London.

2. Will of Mary Hampson,1698, Prob/11/446, National Archives, London.

3. Mary Hampson vs. Charles and Elizabeth Bill, and Mary Hampson,1693.

4. Responses of William Baker, Charles Bill and Elizabeth Bill in Mary Hampson vs. Charles and Elizabeth Bill, and Mary Hampson, 1694, C 9/276/62, National Archives, London.

5. Response of Mary Hampson (daughter), Mary Hampson vs. Charles and Elizabeth Bill, and Mary Hampson, 1694, C 5/164/50, National Archives, London.

6. The archived issues of the *London Gazette* for these years are fairly complete, though one cannot rule out the possibility that the advertisement may have been in an issue that no longer survives.

7. Raveley Fen, Deed of Release,1694, 319/Bundle 15/1, CRO/Hunt, Cambridge-shire Records Office, Huntingdon, UK.

8. Mary Hampson vs. Charles and Elizabeth Bill, and Mary Hampson (1693).

9. Ibid.

10. Responses of William Baker, 1694.

11. Heraldic visitations were carried out from time to time by the College of Arms in order to regulate the use of coats of arms and titles. These visitations also attempted to ensure only those who had the right to call themselves gentlemen and gentlewomen did so.

12. Henry St. George, *The Visitation of the County of Huntingdon, 1684*, ed. John Bedells (London: Harleian Society, 2000), 53.

13. Will of Mary Hampson,1698.

14. Mary Opaven (Uphoven) vs Charles and Elizabeth Bill and Mary Hampson (1698) Prob/18/25/200, National Archives, London.

15. Ibid.

16. Ibid.

17. Sentence regarding the Will of Mary Hampson (1698) Prob/11/448. National Archives, London.

18. Robert Arundel [for Mary Opaven] vs. William Baker (1698) C9/454/122. National Archives, London.

19. Harpson [Robert Hampson] vs John Whalley (1664) C 10/103/65, National Archives, London.

CONCLUSION

1. Letter from Mary Hampson to William Trumbull, April 4, 1681, D/ED/O53, Berkshire Records Office, Reading, UK.

2. These reformists sought to remove all aspects of religious practice that they saw to be based on centuries of Roman Catholic practice rather than Biblical teachings.

3. John Milton, *The Doctrine and Discipline of Divorce* (London,1642, revised 1644), *The Judgment of Martin Bucer* (London, 1644), *Tetrachordon* (London, 1645), and *Colasterion* (London, 1645).

4. Milton, *The Judgment of Martin Bucer*, 17.

5. Ibid., 8.

6. Milton, *The Doctrine and Discipline of Divorce*, 5.

7. Milton, *Colasterion*, 8.

8. Tim Stretton, "Marriage, Separation and the Common Law," in *The Family in Early Modern England*, ed. Helen Berry, Elizabeth Foyster (Cambridge, Cambridge University Press 2007), 33–34.

9. Sharon Achinstein, "Saints or Citizens? Ideas of Marriage in Seventeenth-Century English Republicanism," *Seventeenth Century* 25 no.2 (2012): 253.

10. Dorothy A. Mays, *Women in Early America: Struggle, Survival, and Freedom in a New World* (Santa Barbara, CA: ABC Clio, 2004), 11.

11. Julie Hardwick, "Early Modern Perspectives on the Long History of Domestic Violence: The Case of Seventeenth-Century France," *Journal of Modern History* 78 (2006): 26.

12. Letter from Mary Hampson to William Trumbull, 5 June 1981.

13. Michael Benjamin and Howard Irving, "Money and Mediation: Patterns of Conflict in Family Mediation of Financial Matters," *Mediation Quarterly*, 18.4. (2001): 349.

14. Lauren M. Papp, E. Mark Cummings, and Marcie C. Goeke-Morey, "For Richer, for Poorer: Money as a Topic of Marital Conflict in the Home," *Family Relations* 58 no.1 (2009): 93.

15. Stretton, *Women Waging Law*, 91.

16. There is greater variation in the percentage of women petitioning for divorce in Britain between 1898 and 1944 for a variety of legal and cultural reasons, but after 1944 the frequency of female petitioners for divorce is roughly in line with U.S. figures.